HELP

ii

KATIE HOPKINS
HELP

Published by
KHP Ltd

iv

First published in 2021 by KHP Ltd
Unit 93 Basepoint Business Centre, Yeoford Way, Exeter, Devon EX2 8LB

ISBN 978-1-7371228-1-4

A CIP catalogue record for this book is available from the British Library.

Set in Minion Pro

Cover design © KHP Ltd 2021

HELP: A SURVIVAL GUIDE FOR LIFE

Part autobiography, part comedy, **HELP** is a survival guide for life from Katie Hopkins.

Laugh-out-loud funny, the 'biggest bitch in Britain' lays bare her life, exposing her many private and public failings and how she has survived them.

With tactics for keeping going, new ways of thinking about problems that seem too big to handle, and strategies for coping with unkindness (especially online), **HELP** is here to do just that.

Whether it's your college mates, job, sex life, marriage, kids, or social media that's making you want to shove your head in a blender, **HELP** will give you fresh eyes to see things differently.

Katie Hopkins does not hold back. Loved and loathed in equal measure, she has faced more personal dramas than the Real Housewives – all of them. Because of her uncompromising views, she has faced unprecedented attacks from governments, the media, and the mob.

She was deported from Australia, banned from South Africa, has a fatwa on her head from Pakistan, and the Democrats in America have called on the U.S. Department of Homeland Security to revoke her visa.

She survived a brain surgery that nearly ended her life, she lost a High Court case that cost her the family home, and she was a target of a jihadist plot to behead her.

Hopkins knows how it feels to be floored. But she just keeps getting back up, and she has prevailed. What's more, she still has a sense of humor.

Written in response to all those asking her how she does it, she is on a one-woman crusade to help young people withstand the brutality of the social-media mob or better equip the rest of us to battle our secret demons and step up to a position of strength.

When you really think you can't face your own life anymore, or want to throw yourself on the floor and scream like a 3 year-old in a supermarket, **HELP** will pick you up, dust you off, and get you back on your feet again.

Love her or hate her, this is a must-read for anyone who is struggling. Don't try and cope on your own, reach for **HELP**.

CONTENTS

INTRODUCTION: BEFORE WE START

First, thank you. Thank you for taking the time to find and buy this book. Knowing that no publisher or bookstore would touch a book by Katie Hopkins with a barge pole, I went ahead and wrote and published it anyway. The literary industry is – frankly – scared of its own reflection. If J.K. Rowling is no longer acceptable for refusing to believe men are women, I think we can agree that I am the literary equivalent of anthrax.

My last book, RUDE, involved a lot of over-sharing about my life, encouraging you to laugh along at my mistakes and avoid making them yourself. Despite never making it into a store, it was a bestselling book for my publisher, but he was pilloried by his peers for giving me a platform and daring to make a business profit.

HELP is every bit as brutally honest about my life, but it is written as a handbook for your life, whether you are fed up with being single, sick to death of the Covid madness, plagued by guilt as a mother, or sitting in the Chair of Despair.

For the young, I am hoping it will be like having a mad aunt in your pocket, cheering you on as you try and navigate living a life in the age of social media and Covid.

It's for your single girlfriend who can't find a man (or a hot lesbian), your mate who desperately wants to get married, and your dad who has cancer but doesn't want to talk about it.

I wrote HELP partly because I felt it was what we all needed right now, all of us – however fine we may pretend to be on the outside. And also directly in response to all the thousands of e-mails I get from lonely souls who feel like no one in their own life actually understands them.

Those who contact me often find themselves up late at night writing long e-mails just to unload and know that someone understands, or at the very least that they will not be judged. I am a gateway to at least being heard and, most likely, understood. That is the perfect synopsis of HELP: It is your book, to help you feel less alone. And to stand just that little bit taller tomorrow.

As you will read, I have dealt very badly with many of the worst things that life has thrown at me, and have failed even harder. I see influencers trying to project their perfect lives; I am showing you that mine isn't. If you think you have done something bad, I will almost certainly have done worse. But there are moments of triumph in here, too – I urge you to indulge in the good things in your life.

I should warn more innocent readers that, as with RUDE, the clue is in the title. I do not hold back, I tend to shout, and I am not cautious with my dramas.

I do not have a filter or privacy notice; nor do I have secrets or stuff I hold back. And I certainly do not consider your sensitivity levels. As I like to remind audiences, I do not give offence; you choose to take it. You need to make better decisions.

I know a lot of conservative Americans like to pretend they

have no idea where babies come from, even when surrounded by a blond-haired, blue-eyed mob of their own making, and a husband with a broad smile. But this pretense is not upheld by me.

If the word 'vagina' scares you, you should demand a refund for this book immediately. If my sexual exploits are going to make you chafe in all the wrong departments then, again, please pass this book on to the homeless or the blind. Fifty Shades of Grey was a best-seller for a reason and, my darlings, we all have needs. I just talk more openly about mine than most.

I will warn you that some spellings are British, others are American, and some are in-between. My proofreader has tried to discipline me, but some words just need to be left to fall on the page and feel right the way they are. If you can't get over the fact there are two equally good ways to spell humor, I fear you may well have lost your own.

But if you need a good laugh or find yourself in tears more often than you feel you should, I think you will find the HELP you need here within these pages.

This is me, throwing you a rope and asking you just to keep holding on. At a time when we are losing too many people to dark thoughts, I would love to HELP just one more person pull through.

There is no tiptoeing around the hard stuff: self-loathing, suicide, terminal illness – these are part of my life too. I know this book cannot possibly be the solution to all our problems, but I think it will help you find answers within yourself, just as I have found them within me.

Open it in the way I have opened myself up to you – totally –

and for goodness sake, let me HELP you feel better about your world, even if it's just by laughing at me.

Jump on. Strap in. And let's feel better together.

CHAPTER 1

WHO THE HELL ARE YOU TO HELP ANYONE?

To be clear, I am no one.

I have no medical qualifications, no counselling or psychology certificates.

In fact, you could say the opposite is true.

For most of my life in the public eye I have been seen as the 'Biggest Bitch In Britain' and something of a complete twat (British-speak for dumbass).

A good 50 percent of the population would consider me to be the last person on earth they would come to for help.

Many of the haters have been taught to believe I am a monster… I have been libeled as a drug addict, labelled a racist, and laughed at as an epileptic. Much of what has been written and said about me is wholly untrue.

But I have also given my haters more than enough ammunition to fire at me. There are so many examples of Hopkins 'twattery' for them to use as evidence I can hardly complain when I am criticized. And perhaps, in a world of saccharine sweetness, anyone not delivering a spoonful of sugar with every opinion really is a monster.

'Katie Hopkins is a twat' was approved thought in the UK.

Even when someone found themselves in agreement with me, they would feel the need to preface any agreement with, 'I hate this woman but ... she has a point here.' Or, 'I can't stand this woman ... but ... she is not wrong.'

Perhaps you were one of those people. Do not feel bad. We are entitled to disagree; it is just unfortunate that so many of us have been schooled to think we have to hate those we disagree with. I wonder on what planet people think it is normal to say they can't stand you before speaking? But still.

Love and hate are separate from agreement or otherwise. Increasingly, those in front of the camera rely on saying what their audiences want to hear in order to be liked, and that's a very weird way to decide your own mind.

Being liked was never my goal. I said things as I saw them and grew a massive audience of people who felt their voices were not being heard anywhere else on TV.

Clearly some of my truths proved hard to stomach – like me saying Tyler is a terrible name for a child and that a Tyler can be relied on to be the biting kid other moms dread. It might be an unsavory thing to say, but it remains true.

Many of you will have seen videos of me sitting on a couch next to a particularly large lady, informing her to her face I would not employ her because she is too fat. Again, this directness may offend our sensibilities, but it does not make it any less true.

Regardless, my hard-won title of 'Biggest Bitch in Britain' is under threat.

More and more people are starting to come over to Team Hopkins, or at least starting to see that, with all the madness going on around us, I might actually be one of the only ones speaking some sense – or, at the very least, one of the very few refusing to comply with the insanity being spewed out on a daily basis by the mainstream media (aka MSM). I give a different perspective based on personal strength and individual accountability.

Many of these new supporters are also aware I have been crucified in the media for most of my life. If you are one of them, you will have seen me lose jobs, lose my family home, have a couple of jihadis come for my head, and have social services call for my children. You will have watched me go through it. To quote a Kardashian, 'It's been a lot.'

Happily, despite all the efforts in the public square to terminate my existence, I am still here speaking my unfiltered truths, which is really all I have ever been trying to do. As I write, I am on my second Stand Up Tour of the USA and my audiences appreciate the fact I simply refuse to lie down and die quietly.

Now, I have to acknowledge, it has taken a global pandemic, a national lockdown, utter panic, and the threat of plague and probable death to make people wonder if maybe I am not an asshole –and that's quite something.

It has taken an actual plague for people to realize that I am not a complete twat – quite an achievement by anyone's standards. When I say I was known as the Biggest Bitch in Britain, I was not exaggerating. I was the sort of twat that you can see from space, like the Great Wall of China. I had become the Great Twat of Britain. Perhaps for some of you I still am.

But let's not dwell. Better to be a Great Twat than a dry

one. (*Handy reminder for my American friends: 'twat' is also British-speak for front bottom.)

Honestly, I am not sure how I feel about my own redemption from TWAT to LEGEND or at least LESS OF A TWAT THAN WE THOUGHT.

Courtesy of speaking out against the lockdown madness, I am enjoying something of an awakening of my own, with a whole new audience to speak to and engage with, and I am delighted to have so many new ears and eyes on board.

I welcome anyone who will take the time to listen, and I have this very important assurance for them, too: we do not have to agree. I am not trying to persuade you of my view. I am merely sharing it in the hope that you feel emboldened to share yours in return. That's how conversations were supposed to go before everyone decided they were supposed to think the same thing.

Questions I am often asked:

Q: How do you handle being so hated?

A: I have a system and a process for it. I will share it with you.

Q: Don't you worry for your kids; I mean, aren't they ashamed of you?

A: First, they know the real me, and the real me is a pretty decent person. Second, they know I am not a normal mum. They understand I am doing this for them. And overall, they've seen a bit of what I have had to deal with and overcome and think I pretty much rock and roll.

Q: Do you get attacked in the street?

A: No. Most just come up to shake my hand and say kind

things. Some tell my children they should be proud of me. I milk this for all that it's worth.

Q: Don't you miss your family?

A: I am assuming you want to make me feel guilty or upset. My question to you is: why? Does it make you feel good if I feel less? Of course I miss them. I tell people I work like a husband; it helps them understand.

Q. Can I feel your brain?

A: Yes. I had a third of my skull removed. You can feel my brain and I can move it for you, too.

You know, somewhere along the line, we lost our way. We reached a point where we had to agree in order to get along – that to be liked you had to share the same opinion, and holding opposing views dictated that you called each other a twat.

And all sides are guilty of this, whatever sides or teams you are on – left, right, straight, gay, Christian, Orthodox Jewish, or none of the above. Even news channels are guilty: Pumping out content and contributors who will effectively blow their audiences for clicks, racing down narrow alleyways of opinion together instead of blasting it all out there onto the road and allowing people to decide for themselves.

Endlessly chasing numbers means pleasuring the people who drive them, and truth gets as lost along the way as an Uber driver.

It's why we are surrounded by shallow celebrities who spout the popular opinions, and why reality shows like The Jungle or Celebrity Big Brother lost all of their appeal. When everyone is competing to be liked, no one is willing to be the bad guy and be real.

They say 'just be yourself' with their lip fillers and Botox when every sinew in their inauthentic bodies is straining to be anything but.

Arguably, people are thinking I am not such a twat at the moment because we are agreeing a bit. By that argument, as soon as we disagree again I will be going back into the twat box.

But I prefer not to follow that logic. I don't want this new audience I have acquired to simply bugger off when we start to disagree. I want them to stay and chat, as I prefer to see this as an entry point. I want to embrace everyone recently on the Hopkins Train, even those day riders who may decide to hop off at any point.

Some of you will have been 'with me' for well over a decade, cheering me on through thick and thin, resisting the MSM nonsense and understanding who I am and what I am trying to do. You will always have a special place in my heart, and I thank you for your sheer tenacity and loyalty in supporting my battered self.

Whatever your start point on this journey, we can agree I am a deeply flawed individual and certainly not in a position to offer FDA-approved HELP to anyone. (Thank God for that.)

But together, as a merry band of travelers, we are going to find a way through all of this, and I want to play a part in helping make that happen. I am delighted to have grown an audience that is interested and curious about my life and my views on the world and uses them to feel better about their own.

Let's feel better together.

CHAPTER 2

HELP,
I'M GOING STIR CRAZY

As I sit here jotting away, England is still in lockdown and, if anything, things are getting worse by the day. Australians are not allowed to leave their festering little island or return to it; New Zealanders have just been locked down again and have been told not to speak to their neighbors; and the Premier of Victoria wants his people to drink through their face masks with a straw.

Politicians are currently falling over themselves to stop us from booking a simple summer holiday and make us all as miserable as can be. The main message seems to be that Covid is everywhere, killing everyone, and we should all be in fear of our lives as a result.

However, undaunted by my impending certain death from Covid, I am sitting on a Delta Airlines flight to Fort Lauderdale in search of warm weather and a state where you can still eat inside and speak to people, and the proportion of sane individuals is higher than the batshit-bonkers majority who seem to be roaming the streets everywhere else.

Florida is becoming quite the haven. Not just because the Former-President-Who-Will-Always-Be-My-President-Even-

Though-I-Am-A-Brit legged it to Mar-a-Lago as soon as he left the White House, but because Florida has so many great things – like women with pneumatic boobs and lips, tanned grandparents who are still able to run quite fast in a straight line along the beach, and geckos that fall to earth from the sky when it gets too cold.

I totally empathize with the little critters. If I had the option of just hurling myself out of a tree when the temperature dipped below 90 degrees Fahrenheit, I would absolutely do it. It's as if they are protesting against the insult of being cold, and I feel exactly the same way.

It remains a great mystery why I was born in the UK when I clearly am cold-blooded and require a fairly constant 40 degrees Celsius in order to live my best life. People in Africa seem to complain rather a lot that they don't have access to water or basic sanitation, but stick a Somali in the UK for the winter and they soon realize their life was actually pretty all right before and that having to sleep in socks is a lot harder than looking for a place to take a piss. This week it was minus 23 degrees in Scotland, which helps explain why the Scots are notoriously miserable.

The leader of Scotland, a small ferreting little woman that I call the Ginger Dwarf from the North epitomizes the very worst of what Scotland has to offer: angry ginger people with ego issues. Most Scots are nothing like this miserable mutant, and I am grateful for their love of life and whisky.

As if our miserable weather wasn't testing enough, Covid and lockdowns have been an absolute bloody nightmare in every single way imaginable. I am not saying Covid doesn't exist, but our response to it – and by 'our' I mean our miserable politicians, not decent people like you and me – has been far worse than anything that any seasonal flu had to offer.

Given that I am still somewhat functioning, am not swinging from a tree (as so many others have been forced to do) and am not doubly incontinent and rocking back and forth in isolation like a polar bear in a Chinese zoo, I am clearly enduring this insanity rather well. That said, I had best share my tips for survival with you, dear reader. I would like to have imagined that all of this would be over by now and that lockdowns would have been a thing of 2020 or the past. But something tells me it's all part of the new normal, and sharing my advice feels like it will still be prescient a year from now when this book is in your sticky hands.

And even if you are a subscriber to lockdowns and face masks, your own mother died of Covid, and you are a fully signed-up member of the 'Covid will kill us all' mafia, you will be able to at least accept we think very differently about Covid and understand why I feel the need to uplift those who do not believe the bullsh*t we are force-fed on a daily basis.

I believe Covid is a weaponized virus manufactured by humans in a lab in Wuhan, China and deliberately released to usher in the Global Reset. I believe that leaders across the world were required to comply with this program. And, in return for being complicit in the destruction of our democracies, our economies, and our ways of life, they have been guaranteed a seat at the table of the New World Order government and financial provisions for themselves and their enablers to make this transition.

More personally, those in power have been acting as insider-traders on the vaccine market that they are foisting on their populations, and they will be rewarded financially beyond their wildest imaginations. And their families will become the most powerful ones on the planet in the centuries to come.

Try saying that in public or online, and you will be either marked down as certifiably crazy, obliterated from all knowledge outlets, or arrested and locked up – and, quite possibly, all three! During lockdown in Australia I made a jolly joke about running out of quarantine naked in baby oil and I was deported for my joke. A worrying side effect of Covid is that people have lost their bloody sense of humor, too.

I hold these beliefs because they are the only credible explanation for the complete obliteration of our way of life in response to a virus that is nonlethal for 96 percent of the population and that has a recovery rate of 99.7 percent – and the only possible way to explain why so many uniquely different governments have seemed to march in lockstep, as if working from a common guidebook that none of the rest of us can see.

I am not going to try to persuade you to my point of view; that would be futile. There are two camps here, believers and nonbelievers, and trying to persuade a member of one to cross over to the other would be like trying to persuade a Democrat to love Trump. It just isn't going to happen.

My own family does not agree with me. Against my wishes, my mother and father have had the vaccine – or whatever it was in that syringe supplied by the state. My own sister is a fully paid-up believer and injects other people as part of her job.

In fact, I don't even have an issue with those who worship

at the altar of Covid and kneel down before the mask-enforcers or turn up in full hazmat suits to get on an American Airlines flight from Atlanta to New York to Connecticut.

How other people choose to live their lives is none of my business, and whatever makes them feel most comfortable is what they should do. I just wish they would extend the same courtesy to me.

Below, I illustrate some of the weirdness around the Covid and lockdown insanity, and how I am insulating myself from it.

If lockdowns work, why are we now on the third one?

Britain has made it illegal for people to leave their own homes and has been sending out the Covid-19 Stasi police to harass people in their own cars (just taking a mental break from their own families), has fined kids for having snowball fights, and has sent kids home who were sledding in the snow. If it is fun, you are not allowed to do it. If it was successful, it has been locked down, and if it brought you joy, it has been banished altogether.

If these methods were so effective at controlling the virus, then (a) why do we have to keep doing them, (b) why are countries and states that didn't lock down facing about the same level of Covid cases as states that locked themselves down harder than Alcatraz, and (c) why are we still locking down even when we have fewer hospitalizations and deaths and a massive vaccine program underway?

Australia and New Zealand have taken lockdowns to an extreme. As I type, Prime Minister Jacinda Ardern has locked down New Zealand (the whole country) over a single case of

Covid – a whole country for a single case. It doesn't take an Einstein to work out that if she plans to keep the island clear of any cases, it will never be open again.

Since when were quarantines designed for the healthy?

We can all understand the idea of quarantining the sick. When you think back to the Ebola plague in Africa, which essentially dissolved one's organs from within, no one was arguing that afflicted individuals should be allowed to wander about willy-nilly sputtering their infected blood all over other people because freedom mattered more.

But locking up the healthy is not just overkill; it is something far more sinister – the desire to control people absolutely.

'From' and 'with'

We can all agree that 'from' and 'with' mean two very different things. If I have cancer, I might well die from it. But if I have cancer and a car crash kills everyone inside my car, I didn't die from cancer; I died with it. And so my death should be counted as a death by car crash, not a death from cancer.

Of course, with Covid, all that sensible kind of rationale went out the window. It didn't matter whether you died with Covid or from Covid, or even if you had tested positive for Covid in the last 28 days; your death became a Covid death and was added to the tally.

Auto-cue readers (who like to call themselves journalists) seem to get a weird, fizzy buzzing in their pants when they read out the deaths attributed to Covid and see the numbers rising. They put on that special concerned face that they save for disasters and terrorist attacks, and pretend like they aren't thinking about what's for tea.

I have hundreds of e-mails from children who, like me, feel outraged that their parent's death was used as part of this lie. They tell me that their parent had this or that disease or an underlying health condition, and were baffled when the death certificate listed Covid as the killer.

Where there are lies, there is money.

Hospitals are paid more per Covid death so, naturally, they are incentivized to find more Covid deaths.

The Covid cult

There has been much freakishly cultish behavior associated with Covid.

Face masks are an obvious example, particularly the freaks that not only wear a mask but also a visor. Some have been known to rock up at airports wearing a full hazmat suit as well. It is curious that we can go from being a happy planet that enjoys online dating (where people joyfully have sex with strangers they've just met) to one on which people won't leave the house unless they have themselves cellophaned to their own head – all within the space of just six months.

For the record, I was delighted that people were having lots of sex with strangers and enjoying themselves. If we knew then what we know now, perhaps more of us would have done exactly the same.

'Sky Clapping' is another perfect example of the new cult. Americans and the uninitiated will likely be blissfully unaware that during much of the first lockdown, British people were instructed to go out onto their front doorsteps and clap at the sky at 8 PM on a Thursday night. I am not making this up. British people actually stood on their own doorsteps and clapped meaningfully at the sky.

Ostensibly, the clapping was supposed to be a tribute to our socialized healthcare service (aka the National Health Service or NHS) but, of course, in reality it was a government-led exercise in behavioral compliance. I can almost feel the Behavioral Psychology Unit on Downing Street rubbing themselves up against the corners of their desks in high excitement at how clever they had been, and how easily the plebeians had complied. It worked a treat.

Eager to outdo each other, Brits started getting dressed up for the Sky Clapping, and filming themselves in action. Not to be outperformed, some started coming out with musical instruments to play along for the Sky Clappers. And before we knew it the posher folk of London had full-on operatic performances and a string quartet playing in the better parts of Kensington.

In order to reinforce just how wonderfully behaved the British people are, and how grateful to their socialized healthcare masters and betters, mainstream-media crews were sent to particularly glamorous Sky Clapping locations to capture the moment. People who had dressed their streets with flags or had all come out for socially distanced clapping with champagne were rewarded with a spot on the evening news and a sense of superiority over their less well-performing friends.

In a more sinister turn of events, absentees were noted. Fidel Castro would have been proud. As time wore on, the novelty wore off; when the harsh reality of lockdown really started to bite, fewer and fewer people were turning out for the clapping.

When Mrs. Jones at Number 6 was a no-show for two weeks in a row, the neighbors were very angry and Sky Clappers took to Facebook to wish harm on her family. If you failed to turn out to clap at the sky, neighbors would suggest that you should be denied healthcare or that, if your children were to become sick, they should be refused treatment from the NHS.

This is the reality of socialized healthcare. It is an extension of the strong arm of the state and the brute squad of the left. It meant that, in the UK, the cult of Covid had taken a strong hold.

By the third lockdown, some Sky Clappers had become filled with regret that they were ever taken in by the nonsense and wished they had never shown their faces. Some felt a certain sense of shame that they had been so afraid for themselves and their families, and that they had genuinely felt the NHS was their savior. I don't blame them. They'd been made to feel that way; they were trusting types who had held faith in things like the news, the government and the medical profession.

More terrifyingly, however, was the fact that enthusiastic Sky Clappers still remained. For them, summer evenings spent preparing and self-publicizing their clapping activities were highlights of 2020, and they still reflect fondly on those times, perceiving them as having been representative of national unity against a shared enemy, the virus.

They will never see that the enemy we face is within, and the state will stop at nothing to expand its hold on power.

Covid snobbery

Britain is nothing without its snobbery. Our class system was baked into us long before we emerged pale and plain from the womb, and the class into which you were born always has a firm grip on any other class to which you might aspire.

Of course, the holier-than-thou leftists love the NHS. Many work inside it. It is the brute squad of the British Labour Party. But the liberal elite are the most snobby buggers of all.

Suddenly all of these migrant-loving, NHS-supporting champagne socialists were on chat groups advising each other to avoid the cheaper supermarket chains in case they might 'catch something'.

I swear to God, many of my right-on middle-class friends agreed that they would only be shopping at Whole Foods during Covid because you'd be much less likely to catch it there – as if poorer people are somehow dirtier or more accommodating carriers of the plague. These utter cretins actually believe Covid, despite being a virus, will show the proper respect for the 'better' and 'more informed' classes.

In New York City every restaurant has a notice on its door telling the unvaccinated they are no longer welcome inside the premises. Given that 78% of young black Americans have refused to take the state injectable, the awkward sight of black Americans forced to eat out on the curb while 'educated whites' eat indoors is enough to send shivers down my spine.

No Blacks, No Irish, No Dogs is back. Except this time it's the unvaccinated who are unwelcome. I abhor it with every fiber of my being.

The family policeman

Covid has done nothing for family relations, not only in the sense that we never expected to have to live in the same space 24/7 with our husband, wife or children without work, school or play, but also in the way family dynamics changed.

You may recognize this trait in your own family: One member appoints him or herself as the family policeman and decides for everyone else what they are and are not allowed to do. Mostly are not allowed.

Too many families have endured this experience; someone who is a Covid believer and worshipper, often working inside the healthcare system, appoints themselves the family Covid policeperson and lockdown monitor, and starts to wield power over their elders and betters.

They particularly focus their tyranny on older family members, detailing when they should go out and where and for how long (if at all).

My parents have been told they should stay home, to only go to the supermarket once a week, and under no circumstances to take a bus. They are told they should be taking the vaccine and should not be traveling anywhere. Under no circumstances should they be having any fun.

Similarly, the unclean and unvaccinated family members are uninvited from Thanksgiving, funerals and Christmas in case they spread this bonkers plague on to the more elevated members of the family.

I know so many parents whose own children no longer speak to them because they refuse to get the jab.

This is another form of control. For me, there's the added

twist that, if my mum or dad should get Covid, I will somehow be to blame; I will have killed them both. The family Covid policeperson will make sure that I know it, too.

When the cure is worse than the cause

This is a harder argument to make because, of course, the quiet misery of millions and the private act of suicide lack the drama and sound effects of one elderly individual suffocating on a ventilator courtesy of Covid. And, frankly, I never want to see or hear any of these things.

But if the rate of suicide is to be believed, combined with the unnecessary deaths from undiagnosed or untreated cancers and God-knows-how-many-other deaths caused by sheer loneliness, loss of resilience and natural defenses, and the cruel isolation of elderly in nursing-care homes, I would argue that the cure is worse than the cause – particularly as deaths from the cure affect the young and new parents.

I have been overwhelmed with letters from individuals who simply do not want to go on living their life if this is what it is going to be like. These are not the words of the mentally unstable; they are rational thoughts from sane citizens who just don't want to live a life of unkindness and control. I worry I can't say enough of the right things to keep them with us, and I rage at the silence of the mental-health mafia who could not stop talking about it in the past and now appear to have been struck dumb.

How many elderly people do the Covid police really expect to come out of lockdown and survive? Reduced mental capacity, reduced muscle strength, reduced physical resilience, a deficient immune system – and all for what? Just to say that they endured another year on the face of this planet? Puhleeze! Give me gin and morphine, and just let me go.

Thinking about these questions has been an integral part of how I've survived lockdown when, frankly, all I really wanted to do was inflict acts of violence on a daily basis. Well, thinking about these questions , buggering off to America under the guise of work, drinking a lot of Merlot, and running like an Ethiopian on acid.

I also have a range of obnoxious behaviors I like to call on to lift my spirits when things get to be a little too much. On a scale of 1 to 'you absolute twat', I aim for the latter and encourage you to do the same for your own entertainment and to get you through the day. You score five points for each of the following that you manage to achieve:

- Hover near the hand-sanitizer unit in a store, wait for someone to use it, and casually remark that you heard it had been filled up with sperm.
- Sneeze. But, instead of 'A-chew!', try shouting 'Covid!' or 'Corona bollocks!' This is not only good for twat points but sharpens your mental dexterity as well.
- Lick a door handle and walk out singing songs from the movie Frozen. No one will bother you, I promise.
- Smother someone in a line or queue. And then pretend to be terribly sorry at their outrage.
- Pick up groceries and put them back on the shelf under the watchful eye of the Covid police.
- Get a T-shirt with a gun on it, take off your mask, and boldly walk around with a face that says, 'Don't f*ck with me!' Most

people won't.

- Gesture to someone alone in a car with their mask on that they are alone in the car with their mask on. Just as you would if they didn't have their headlights on at night. Both things are equally stupid.
- When someone asks whether you have had the vaccine, talk about your vagina in detail. When they look surprised, thank them for being so interested in all your private medical issues. Make physical contact with them before you waft off.
- Be more weird than them. If someone says to you: 'Don't worry, I'm double-jabbed,' offer them a random fact about yourself in return: 'I won Best Cake in Show at the Country Fair.' Two can play at the game of sharing random facts.

For the purposes of avoiding litigation or having this book sacrificially burned by the Arch-alien Chris Whitty (the British government's chief scientific adviser), let me remind you that I am not a doctor, have no medical qualifications, and am not trusted to be a godparent to any of my children's friends, let alone dispense health-related advice.

In my defense, I am 46 years old, 5 feet 8 inches tall, weigh 130 pounds, and can outrun most men, so when it comes to the practical stuff that matters, I am virtually a frickin' Dr. Anthony Fauci – except taller and hotter, and I've had sex this year with someone other than myself.

Most importantly of all, let's try to remember individual choice. It is not a problem if people want to act weird, be Covid believers, or lock themselves away; that is their choice, and they should live however makes them most comfortable.

But you are not them. Their choices are not yours. And they have no right to try and impose their beliefs on you.

The cult of Covid is exactly that. And if you haven't chosen to enter that particular church, its worshippers should have the decency and good sense to leave you alone.

You do you. Let me do me.

Sometimes, our very best defense is to live each day just as free as we can be.

CHAPTER 3

HELP,
I'M BEING BULLIED

When you are known as the Biggest Bitch in Britain, or portrayed in the media as a monster, many assume you are a Teflon-dipped queen, impervious to hurt. You are no longer a person with a name, you are just a name to be abused – hard and repeatedly.

It is odd of course, because most of those calling me terrible names or wishing me dead have never met me. They have no idea who I actually am; they just hate the idea they have of me. And my name is a vent for their anger, like a sh*t funnel in a sewage plant.

After 15 years or so in the public eye, I must have been called just about every name under the sun – and, as is so often the case with unkindness online, much of it focuses on my face.

My face is often used as a kind of reference point for evil. There are memes with me as the White Chicks, with a penis for a nose; as various horses; as ugly birds; or as strange-looking fish.

There are more obvious comparisons: how much I look like Boris Becker (I really do) or, less kindly, like Iggy Pop (I see that too). But apparently I also look like Margaret Thatcher in a certain light – which feels like a compliment, even if she was 65 years old at the time. Given my accent and my face, Americans often think I look like Princess Anne – but I'm pretty happy with that as she is a tough old bird too, albeit twice my age and a great deal better at horse riding.

This is a popular insult: 'Hopkins, you horse-faced cow, I wouldn't piss on you if you were on fire!'

I do wonder about that expression. If I were on fire, I very much doubt I would actually want anyone to piss on me at that precise moment. I feel a foam-based fire hydrant or a blanket might be more useful. Even in my sexual past, I never found the thought of being pissed on very alluring, though I know many others who do. I have gossip on this if you would like to hear it. It involves Piers Morgan.

This is another classic: 'Look! (Insert name of elderly relative or older famous person) is five years older than Katie Hopkins. Hate ages you.' And then they put our two photos side by side, one of someone looking fabulous … and me, looking 95.

Weirdly, other women then join in and do the same. They post their favorite picture of themselves looking particularly lovely one day next to one of mine where I look bloody awful, and say, 'I am 16 years older than Katie Hopkins' – so all of their mates can pile on and give them a compliment about how marvelous they look.

I understand what they are doing, and I see that it makes them feel better about themselves. And I am actually kind of happy for them for that. I want women to feel great, genuinely I do.

But it is almost as if they have forgotten I am a real person seeing this. Or as if, because we disagree on a subject, it's okay to make themselves feel better at my expense. I can honestly say I wouldn't want anyone to ever do to them what they do to me.

I genuinely don't want to make another woman feel ugly or old to make myself feel better. It wouldn't, and it's really odd behavior. Like women who like to watch their fat friend eating cake because it makes them feel less guilty about what they're eating. As I tell my children, women can be bloody odd.

If I were ever to bother trying to defend myself from this particular game, I would point out that the famous person, or whoever is being held up as the fountain of youth, clearly got to select a picture of themselves that they were happy with. Your 55-year-old mum, for example, wouldn't share a picture in which she looks rough as a badger's ass; she'd post the most flattering and complimentary one she could find.

I understand this. And I totally see the point/joke they are making. But I don't get the luxury of choosing which picture of me they use.

I also wonder if they have considered for one moment how they would feel if someone did the same to them and posted it on a public forum for their friends to see. They would be mortified, and I'd feel for their hurt.

Sometimes I think I would like to challenge these women to do the same photo comparison with a full-body shot. Let's stick a bag on our heads and compare naked photos side by side, and see who looks younger then.

I say this because my body is ageing more slowly than the rest of me, and because I take comfort in imagining that my critics are eating like horses and probably have thighs that chafe. The thought of chafing thighs makes my neck hair stand on end. Any woman who has to Vaseline her own fat folds to take a walk has probably left it a bit late – just saying.

Chubby people do tend to have excellent skin; a fat layer does tend to push out wrinkles. But if a physician were asked to measure who has the younger body, I reckon I would win every time.

But this is not the answer; in fact, it is the very opposite. This is just looking at their actions and doing something equally self-loathing and hurtful, when in fact the whole behavior needs to be stopped.

I accept that if I am in the public eye and giving my opinion of others, I have to expect others to return the favor, in potentially less than flattering tones. If you put yourself out there you cannot only expect compliments in return and, in the absence of a smart response, a jibe about one's looks is the easy option.

Nevertheless, the level and the noise of these personal attacks has sometimes been extreme, to the point of shocking even my critics, who can see that the hashtag #BeKind was never extended to include me.

Those who now see my softer side might wonder how I have been able to withstand it all. Many thought it was okay when they believed I was a monster; now when they see I am just like them or, at least, that I have a big heart, they are a bit disturbed by what I have been through.

People are shocked when they meet me in real life, like they can't actually wrap their head around the fact I am not so terrible-looking as to curdle milk. Or that I am a smiley thing.

I look at their surprise and see the distance between who they thought I was and who I really am.

I want to share with you how I handle it, in the hope that you might find it helpful in handling any hurt you might feel. If you are one of the people who has called me 'horse face' or 'ugly cow' in the past, please do read on. We aren't always the best versions of ourselves and that is OK.

I once accidentally texted my own nanny – from my own garden, while she was standing in my own kitchen – that she was a fat, lazy cow. I then had to go inside and tell her she was about to receive a text from me calling her a fat, lazy cow. I remain ashamed of myself to this day.

I don't want this to be all about me, either. I am just one example of what so many of us feel every day.

So many of you will look at a picture of yourself and only see the negative or something to criticize. I watch you take a selfie and immediately look at yourself, finding the faults in your face, or your hair, or your size. It breaks my little heart when I see you as funny, or charming, or full of life.

You are doing the haters' job for them, throwing unkindness at yourself. And it's a habit we pass down the line to our children.

How many pictures will a young girl get their mum to take before she finds one that passes muster to post for their friends?

I watch the way groups of friends review a group shot, each person magnifying their own face to see how they look, oblivious to the fact this was supposed to be about capturing a happy group moment and was never about one person's face or their hair.

I should add that none of this is some kind of weird, reverse-psychology exercise in which I tell you all this hideousness about myself in order for you to reassure me I am a MILF (Mother I'd Like to F*ck) and very beautiful indeed.

Plenty of men and women are kind enough to say lovely things to me, which I appreciate. So many tell me I am much better looking in person (not sure what that says about my photos), and many offer to take me into a dark cupboard and do bad things to me, which is also very sharing of them, if a little over-excitable.

One man at a conference asked if he could take me home and bang me harder than a pile-driver working sand. I didn't take him up on the offer but admired his confidence and sense of determination. He has what my buddy Roger Stone would call Big Dick Energy.

A Muslim gentleman – we shall call him Mohammed, as most are – was very cross with himself for having sexual thoughts about me, from a video on Instagram. I informed him Allah would not be amused and he should get out more. My vagina is definitely not halal, nor do I want it to be.

I know I have a certain something about me that some men and women find attractive. And I am thankful beyond measure my husband is still good enough to think I am pretty – even when I know there are many mornings on which I look rougher than a drunk in a bush.

Then again, an Uber driver once came to pick up his ride outside a hotel in Arizona where I was also waiting for a car, and shouted out the window at me: 'Steve? Are you Steve?' I mean Holy Cow, I knew I looked rough that day, but Steve?

Professional colleagues helping to edit and proofread this

book urged me to delete this chapter. They felt it was intrinsically sad and loaded with hurt. They don't like to see me this way or to hear me put myself down like this.

I am so grateful for their kindness, and I am certain they are right. But if I am not exposing myself here, what am I? If my hurt shows through, maybe it will help someone else feel a bit less alone with theirs.

Because the fact remains that even if my face has been the butt of more jokes than Prince Andrew, it serves a purpose here in HELP. By sharing how it has been for me, there will be things that you will know are true for you too. Sharing what it is like to be made to feel ugly online is the first step to helping ourselves get through it.

I am compelled to state, however, that whatever you have going on with your face, things are a bit different for me.

People first came to know me when I was much younger (28 years old) and largely benefitting from professional makeup artists and staged pictures shot in studios. Apprentice Katie Hopkins was quite baby-faced in retrospect, and that is the face most people remember. Twenty years on, I am older … and, having been 'ridden hard and put to bed wet', I look older too.

I am older and I look older – and I'm living in a time when women are not supposed to do that. See Jennifer Lopez and her endless bonkfest with Ben Affleck for details. See also Tilda Swinton (I love her) and Goldie Hawn (the sexiest woman on the planet). I love these ladies very deeply indeed.

I also look and seem older than my years. It is a great mystery that my face looks like it has lived two decades longer than my birth certificate says it has. It's as if my face ages in dog years while the rest of me can more or less hold its own as a fit 46-year-old. And living with an older face can be tricky.

Lovely ladies at lunches think I am the same age as them – retired and in their 60s. I never like to embarrass them by admitting I am 15 years younger than they are but have simply lived twice as fast. So I play along as if I were actually around for the Beatles and the first moon landings. I was not.

And when older ladies confide in me about their personal problems – anything from incontinence and lack of sex drive to chafing labial folds – I am required to nod and be sympathetic because they assume I am suffering from the same. (Now, come to mention it, I do have a few of these issues.)

Online, things are much rougher, because people online are often intentionally cruel. Observing that people are nasty bastards online doesn't make it better; nor does it make you feel better when they say something unkind. But it is always worth remembering there is a difference between 'online' and 'real life'. The more time you spend in the latter, the better off you will be.

Newspapers also play a role in all of this. Their idea is to use the worst picture possible in order to support their argument that I am more evil than Chairman Mao. If it's the Mirror, the Guardian, VICE, Huff Po, BBC or Channel 4, the game is to find a picture in which I look like a Bond villain without a cat and use that I probably killed the cat in question.

The photo used most often is one of me in full meringue – wearing my first wedding dress to a Conservative Party conference in order to highlight the need for a quickie divorce from Europe (i.e. Brexit). The picture in question makes me look like a turkey that has been hung by the neck for a good week and then punched repeatedly in the eyes.

The panel I was speaking on was by far the most successful item at that Tory conference. The room was full to overflowing, and it was voted by the audience as the most entertaining event of the day. But, of course, none of this was reported.

Walking into the Conservative Party conference in a massive wedding dress was a pretty ballsy thing to do when everyone else was a stuffed suit busy rubbing their crotch up against a junior minister in the hope of being promoted to rubbing-post-in-chief. Nearly all were gay men pretending to be straight for the purposes of career progression. And all of said suits were bought at John Lewis.

There are other, more flattering pictures that show I didn't look too shabby for a bird who had traveled to Manchester, slept in some random hotel, and changed in a bathroom cubicle across the road into a massive frock twice the size of the toilet itself. I also wonder how many women could actually fit into their first wedding dress ten years after the event.

But trying to defend yourself against pure unkindness is a futile exercise. It's the equivalent of having diarrhea sprayed at you; you're going to get covered in shit no matter what you do. The only things you can be responsible for are your own actions and your responses to theirs.

Criticism of looks and appearance is just part and parcel of being online and living with social media. There are ways to deal with it that leave you in better shape than many young people who are dealing with it now. Nothing is more concerning than watching some poor, bedraggled parent being handed a phone by their child and expected to take repeated photos of him or her pulling a variety of ridiculous faces and poses.

Once, at a restaurant, all five members of my family watched as two parents were handed phones and, for the next ten minutes, obliged to take photo after photo of their two girls and a ridiculous French bulldog clearly purchased for his Instagram-ability.

What is this weird behavior that kids have trained their parents into? The kids snatch back the phones, scan through the pictures at warp speed and, if there are none that make them look the way they want others to imagine them, they shove the phones back into the parents' hands with a surly grunt and expect them to repeat the process. It's such a strange thing to watch, from surly horror to preening teen in the blink of an eye, real life versus online life. And the parents comply!

What are these parents thinking? Just hand back the bloody phones and say no! And why do kids not see the harm they are doing to themselves? Endlessly scanning, posing, deleting, filtering and posting – for what? A click of approval to tell you that you look okay? For friends and strangers to message that you look beautiful? Or be envious of what you appear to have?

What human emotion is this replacing; what void is this filling?

Before smartphones and the internet, where did we get this sense of self-worth or whatever this is? Where did we get our compliments, or show ourselves and have people say we looked terrific, or make us feel great about ourselves, or give us the little boost we needed? These things certainly weren't found by repeatedly taking pictures of ourselves.

The truth is, we found our self-worth out and about in the

real world. Who told me I was great at 14? Or made me feel wanted or attractive? I could list their names now (Matt, Mark, Chris, Rich, Neil…); real boys and a few men whom I knew and with whom I had brushed skin at one time or another, making them want to know me.

Perhaps some didn't want more than 20 minutes of grubby pleasure, but most stuck around for three or four years and were a happy part of my life. There were dads who found me at summer camp and became a side kick to my American adventures; there were music teachers who tried their best to be more than that; there were married men who should have known better but thankfully did not; and there were young lads who I decided would be mine and made it so. There were moments of madness, bursting into bars and kissing men randomly at will. Those were fine times. I fear these fine times don't exist in the same way for young people anymore.

Where will our young girls learn that confidence now? What young teen could actually call a boy on a phone so they can whisper quietly to each other for hours? Or call someone up and ask them to go for a walk? Most avoid an actual phone call like the plague – too intimate, too close, too focused on each other. Something huge has been lost or, more correctly, taken from the young by life online.

I am sad that young people don't have much real, physical reassurance in their lives anymore. Or, at least, I regret the extent to which it has been replaced by this online mania to appear whatever 'perfect' might be.

But feeling sad about it isn't helping anyone, and criticizing isn't helping either. This is the world that kids are in, and the advice that matters is how to deal with our new reality, not how to mourn the old.

I am testament to the fact there is a way to get through all of it – the unkind, the mean, and the downright cruel. And these aren't empty words; these are the ways I have endured it – all of it. These are the tricks I use to process it. These are the ways to get through it – because I am here to show you that you will.

Lessons on how to handle nasty bastards

- Breathe in and out. You will hear this many times over the course of HELP: when you have no idea what to do next, breathe in and out. And keep doing it. Make it the thing you are doing and make no apology for it. It is not a little thing; it is everything.
- Repeat to yourself that you are not responsible for the actions of others. You are only responsible for yourself. Your actions, your responses – nothing else. What someone else does to you or behind your back sits with them. They have to own their unkindness. Take no part of it as your own.
- When someone has made you feel bad about yourself or hurt you, imagine physically sticking the comment back onto them. Imagine writing it on a post-it note and sticking it to their head (although I appreciate you might want to stick it up their ass). See them wearing what they have said or done. Make them own that unkindness and know it does not belong to you. It belongs to them.
- Sometimes people ask questions intended to hurt you. Remember, you don't have to answer a question just because you were asked it, even by 'a friend'. Don't answer. If their

question is asked to exploit your suffering, make them own it. Make others own their unkindness before you take it on as yours. Friends can be the cruelest of enemies, and they get away with it because they wear the 'friend' label like camouflage. When terrible things have happened in my life, these types tend to ask, 'Was it really awful, are you okay?' What they mean is, 'Tell me the gossip so I can pass it on to my mates.' Resist filling them up with your struggles.

- Nothing is 'water off a duck's back'; some things can't be laughed off. Being told to 'just ignore it' is about as helpful as being told to knit yoghurt. When your mind is full of only this one thing that someone said about you, there is not a chance in hell you can just ignore it. You have to acknowledge that it hurts and understand why it hurts. And then, make a deal with yourself to draw a line under it and put it away. If you feel it fraying the edges of your tired head again, you have to repeat this step.

- When something upsets you, ask yourself why, what it is that has really upset you. Keep asking 'so what?' until you get to the crux of the thing. Maybe you are jealous, maybe you are envious, maybe you feel left out. It is unlikely these will be feelings you want to admit to or acknowledge, but you need to be honest with yourself before you can make yourself feel better. The trick is to try and get to the honest bit as quickly as you can.

- Until you have properly processed hurt, you cannot put it away. Your goal is to become the Most Efficient Processor of Hurt that you can be. Understand what it is that has actually upset you, process your hurt like a mofo, and then put it away.

- Have a physical place to put all your hurt – like a box, a bin, or a cat-litter tray. Being able to visualize yourself dealing with this stuff is a really important part of feeling better, and physically putting hurt away can help you remember you are letting this go and giving yourself a break. You need to work hard to give your head a break. It takes effort, but it is effort you need to make.

- Ask yourself how you separate yourself from the unkindness. It's all very well being an Efficient Processor of Hurt, but it cannot mean you stand there asking for more. Sometimes the people we call friends are not. Sometimes we simply try to have more friends to feel better, when in fact fewer would achieve that much more effectively. It is possible that there are friends in your life who you would be happier without.

- There are five people you need in your life; this is the Rule of Five. These can change; one might be your boss or the lady down the road with the dog you wave at in the mornings. It might be your mum or your mate from school. If you have five (5) people you can trust, you are doing well. Even if you have just one, you are very lucky. And if you are sad, despondently thinking that there is no one in your world, you have me.

- Remember, everyone's opinion doesn't carry equal weight. Do not try to award the same merit to the unkindness of a stranger as you would to one of your trusted few. Why would you give credence to the opinions of idiots you don't even know? Chances are, the people who you trust the most are those who love you most of all. And they think you are simply splendid.

- Look at your phone as if it were a monster. It's easy to handle monsters in daylight but ask yourself why you would bring one into your bedroom? Why are you letting people take away your power? Leave the monster in the kitchen at night. You are the boss, you are the owner, you can engage with it on your terms. Do not let your phone be the boss of you.

- Find something that makes you feel good and do much more of it. Long showers, shaving your legs, fake tanning, conditioning your hair, getting a massage, buying a beautiful book – whatever little things make you feel good, promise yourself you will do them much more.

- Create a 'hurt exchange'. When something hurts you, and you are beginning to process it away, exchange it for something that makes you feel good – a framed photo of a time when you felt free, a call with a friend, a glass of Merlot. (I shouldn't advocate drinking but a glass of wine is a good hurt exchange for me, so I had best share it.)

- Me. You have me. I may be many very bad things, but I am proof that you can endure this because I have endured it too and found a way through. And, funnily enough, even my harshest critics and those who find me very ugly indeed are gracious enough to acknowledge that this is true.

- Put a post-it note in this section. Read it when you are struggling and it will pull you through.

Endurance is a very beautiful thing. Go on, my darlings, you can endure this and so much more.

CHAPTER 4

HELP, UNI? YES OR NO?

My mother always said it was unseemly to beg. But here I am, imploring you to consider anything but attending university.

I am fully prepared to throw myself naked at your feet, grab your ankles, and clamp down on them like a crab with a spasm so you are forced to drag my aged (and increasingly odd-looking) body along behind you onto campus.

Trailing the corpse of Katie Hopkins around with you is not the first impression you want to make as you try to befriend the lefties you'll find there, but the image does give you an indication of the lengths to which I am prepared to go to save you from wasting your life at university.

And if I can persuade just one student to do anything but university, it will be worth it. As I write, another generation of students is celebrating exam results and firm offers. Others are about to go through the hideous process of 'clearing' to try to get a university offer at some godforsaken institution desperate for your cash.

British universities have become an extremely lucrative industry. The more kids they process through their doors, like cheap sausages in a meat factory, the greater their profits will be. The more kids they accept, the healthier their bottom line. 'Get a degree!' they say. 'You will learn more, earn more, and live a better life.'

Except they lie.

On what planet is starting out with £60,000 of debt a rational decision? And even if you hit me with the sulky-faced, 'Yeah, but I am never going to pay it off,' I still ask: what the hell is the point in going to uni? £9,000 a year, plus accommodation costs, only to roll out the door three years later with a 2:1 that every other kid has got.

If you aren't different from the rest, what makes you employable? And if you are about to say your personality, then go out into the world and show it off, my love – get three years ahead of your mates. If you still feel like you missed out, you can always go later when you have thought it through (you will never go to uni – I guarantee it).

British kids are now preparing to return to universities under Covid regulations. Vaccine mandates are all about, social distancing has crucified in-person lectures, and most face-to-face contact is curtailed. Universities are online, but on campus – it makes about as much sense as Kamala Harris in the White House.

During lockdown students were obliged to continue paying their fees (£9,000 per year), paying rent on empty flats (even though they were obliged by the government to leave campus and return home), and studying for their degree in isolation without ever going onto campus or attending a lecture.

One medical student, whose course committed him to 500 hours of practical learning in the lab, has only completed two hours, and yet his fees and costs have not been reduced.

In any other business, this would be seen to be grossly unfair, and refunds and recompense would rightly be demanded. Imagine booking a holiday and finding out you only had two nights' accommodation instead of the 14 nights you had paid for. No one would stand for it!

But somehow, because these are 'only students' and universities cling to the facile notion that they are a worthwhile endeavor akin to doing voluntary work or some charitable effort, they can and do get away with anything they choose. Personally, I hope that lockdown and the crippled economy bankrupt many more of these dark places that feed off the young, and that they are wiped from the face of the UK.

But it's not just locked-down universities that make no financial or emotional sense. In 'normal' life, whatever that looks like since the advent of Covid, going to university to get a degree, for the majority of young people, is about as dated a notion as the fax machine. (If you don't know what a fax machine is, you clearly still have the skin elasticity of a 5-year-old. You probably don't know what an LP is, either. I sound like a chuffing grandma. Google 'fax machine', for goodness sake!)

Unemployment rates are highest for kids with useless degrees, a surprising fact that shouldn't be. Many kids still believe that getting a degree will put them ahead of the competition. It's a legacy idea held over from the times when hardly anyone went to university and it was a really aspirational thing to want for your children. My own parents never went to university, and so naturally their aspiration was for me and my sister to go.

In the early 1980s it was a sign that your family had made it in some way, that you had broken out of your working or lower-middle-class background and shoved your kids upwards to a place you could only have dreamed of. I still remember it being a really big deal when my sister went off to uni and the family's pride at this momentous event.

My father grew up in a council house, managed to get to grammar school and, by working all his life in the same job to afford private schooling for his kids, managed to get his first child into a decent university so she could have a better job for life. Many families would proudly tell the neighbors that their child was 'the first [insert family name] to go to university'. I know mine did.

Universities in the 1990s represented hope, aspiration, and parental pride, and the competition to get in felt very real. Being rejected meant you didn't get to go to university, not simply that you had entered clearing and would instead be going to some half-baked institution that would accept a potato if it could pay the fees.

Then along came Prime Minister Tony Blair who, two years into office, declared at his September 1999 conference that 50 percent of British kids should go to university – a random figure pulled straight out of his politician's ass as a symbol of how he was going to bust through the class system in Britain.

'Today, I set a target of 50 percent of young adults going into higher education in the next century,' Mr. Blair told his Labour Party delegates. Behind that political grandstanding came some deeply unpleasant realities. Britain henceforth committed to sending 50 percent of its kids to university regardless of whether

the young person:
- was smart enough to go
- knew what they wanted to do in life
- could afford it
- actually wanted a degree
- would have a job to go to afterwards
- would be rewarded for their investment by the labor market
- would actually be building a better life for themselves.

Blair achieved his aim. Figures from the Department of Education for 2017—18 show that 50.2 percent of people went into higher education; the figures are higher for women, with 57 percent having headed off to get a degree. That figure is likely far higher in 2021.

The rapidity of this growth is only part of the story. In 1980 only 15 percent of the population was in full-time education after the age of 18; that is, in any kind of training or further/higher education, including all universities and what were then called polytechnics. By 1990 that figure had risen to 25 percent for all forms of post-18 education and, by 2020, a full 52 percent of kids were in university, exactly as Mr. Blair had planned, whether or not that was the right thing to do.

If we take each of these 'whether or nots' in turn, it quickly becomes clear how one politician's moment in the limelight has translated into generations of students being conned into the utter scam that is university education in the 2020s.

Are you smart enough to go or not?
Against the old metric of 15 percent of kids heading off to

university, something had to change to enable 50 percent to make it through that door. And it did: standards fell. Not only did they fall – they dropped through the floor.

Soon, universities had to offer essay-writing classes for students because so many arrived from underperforming schools unable to write properly, despite having been awarded high grades in their A-level classes. University lecturers talk of trying to grade essays by those barely able to speak English or understand basic math. League-table culture means that academic staff are under pressure to pass students who should rightfully fail and to award higher classes of degrees to the undeserving.

Lower-grade offers are made to non-European students, who pay even higher fees, to ensure future market share.

Profit is king at British universities. Dullards who can barely scrape together a single D at A level, even under the lax grading standards, can go to university if they are willing to pay. Put simply, you can go to university if you can sign on the dotted line.

As a result, and rightfully so, British universities are slumping in the rankings. In 2012, 62 out of 84 UK universities saw their world rankings downgraded for the fourth consecutive year, according to the Quacquarelli Symonds university rankings.

This is not a criticism of people who are thick or terminally stupid. I am as thick as a fat bird when it comes to physics, so much so that the mere sound of (former D Ream pop star turned astrophysicist) Brian Cox's voice makes my sphincter clench tight.

Being thick in some departments is nothing to be ashamed

of; it just means you're going to be a sparkling diamond in others. What I absolutely object to is kids who could be diamonds in the real world being packed off to university for no reason, where they are forced into being duller than charcoal and half as useful.

Do you know what you want to do or not?

Given that most young people have no clue what they want to do at the best of times, and most have been quite happy getting £20 off mum or dad every time they leave the house (which, under lockdown, is not often), they have no concept of work or what they wish to do with their lives.

Rather than acknowledge that fact and accept the grim reality that they are still at home dependent on their parents, they head off to university. Because what else are they going to do? Doing something is better than doing nothing, right?

Wrong, because that is not an honest question.

Doing something is better than doing nothing, of course, but those aren't the real options here. The real options are Going to University (when you have no clue what you are going to do) versus Trying to Get a Job. Doing nothing should never have been in play.

And I know one seems easier. Going to university is what 'everyone is doing', after all. But even that should cause you to raise an eyebrow. Take a look around at some of your mates who are planning to go to university. Do you really think it's worth them paying £9,000 a year? Will they really benefit?

And I totally understand that in the new Covid-crazy world everything is smaller, harder, more claustrophobic, more confined. You can rightly argue that at least university is a change of scene and allows you to live somewhere different, and I have every sympathy with that urge. I'd have chewed my own arms off if I were confined at home for as long as most have been these past years.

But my question is still, why uni? What is it you want to achieve?

Getting out of home? Why not get a random job in a new city, rent a tiny room, and see what life feels like living it alone? Why not get a job where all of that is taken care of – Disney or Holiday Resort?

Being somewhere else? Just go.

Needing a degree to do the job you want to do? Start at the entry point and see if you still need that piece of paper after three years.

Why not just do anything but uni?

Can you afford it or not?

The average graduate with a three-year degree walks out of university £50,000 in debt plus an interest rate of at least 6 percent. This fact is conveniently avoided by students as they are reassured it is in effect a loan they will never pay off.

This is, in fact, a form of coercion. It is a con-job. These 'uni-recruiters' are worse than car salesmen pushing personal-finance options, or drug pushers; at least with them you end up with a car or drugs.

Young people deserve the respect of being treated like adults, of being told clearly and openly that they are signing up for £50,000 in debt, a debt that will follow them all their lives, increasing all the while – even when they are unemployed or earning just the minimum wage. It will be there if they try to get financing on anything – a house, a car, a holiday – and it will be there when they try to borrow money in the future. It's one of the greatest scams of all time, hiding in plain sight.

A cursory glance at the salary-and-incentive package being enjoyed by the vice chancellor of the business masquerading as a university tells you everything you need to know about where your money is going. It's not to academics or lecturers per se but to the guys at the top plundering the hopes of kids to deliver profit to investors and their own pension pot.

Do you actually want a degree or not?

When Prime Minister Tony Blair stood on his podium and mandated that 50 percent of British kids should go to university, did anyone stop to ask whether that's what the kids want to do? Has anyone asked a school leaver, 'Why do you want a degree?', and asked him or her to really think about it?

'So I can get a job' is easily disproven.

'So I will have better opportunities' does not play out for the majority.

'Because everyone is' might be the most honest answer. And, if everyone is doing it, what singles you out?

My advice: get three years ahead of your mates, debt free.

Will you have a job to go to afterwards, or not?

Australia is well ahead of us on this one. Its government has amended the pricing of degrees in the humanities, social sciences, and law. To enroll in courses such as history and philosophy, Australian students will have to pay more than their peers studying the sciences, mathematics, or healthcare.

In the case of history, for example, the government has proposed that course fees would rise by 113 percent. The cost of many science-related courses would fall by 20 percent, with the cheapest courses now mathematics and agriculture, where fees have decreased by 62 percent.

Pricing kids out of university courses appears to be the only way to make them understand that jobs are simply not there for these disciplines. Or at least, if there is to be a financial reward in the longer term, you will be able to see it and pay for it upfront.

Are you actually building a better life for yourself or not?

I spent three years on campus for my degree. I was paid to be there by the British Army, was on campus before the Covid nonsense, and had Freshers Week, more club nights than decent dinners, and a suspected case of impetigo by term two.

But despite my very best efforts to entertain myself, and somehow passing Advanced Statistics and getting the Adam Smith Award for Economics, I was bored out of my tiny tree after two years and did not graduate with any sense of achievement or pleasure; there was more of a desperate urge to finally get going in life.

I remember my graduation day with a weird feeling of detachment. I could see all the other families looking pleased and proud. Kids I had seen around the uni were there in their gowns and hats, taking pictures here and there. And my own parents were good enough to get all dressed up and take me out for lunch. But I remember it a bit like being on anesthetic; I wasn't really there, and my heart was long gone.

I am not saying I didn't have fun, or show my bottom to the Vice Chancellor (who came back for a second look, by the way), or wake up in places I really shouldn't have, but it was all a bit protracted, even back then. If I were paying close to £50,000 for the pleasure, I would have been weeping at the madness.

There are calls now to reduce maximum tuition fees from £9,250 per year to £7,500 per year and extending repayment over 40 years, with any unpaid amounts cancelled thereafter – which all sounds like window dressing to me.

How exactly is this helping students to build a better life for themselves? Kids attending university today will still be paying back their student loans in their 70s, debts accumulated as we head into the darkest recession in living memory and an era of mass unemployment. What ungodly purpose does that serve?

If you are a young person reading this book because some bonkers uncle has thrust it under your nose and made you look at it, you may be thinking, 'What an old cow she is.' You may be asking yourself, 'What right does this horse-faced old bat have to tell me anything or to shatter my dreams of going to university and becoming a lawyer?'

And you would have a point. I have no right to tell you anything.

But I do have a sense of how the world is shaping up for you right now, and I see the tsunamis of unemployment and recession headed our way. The first waves are already on the shore.

I want you to be the first ones into the lifeboat, crafting it, building it, staying afloat, and helping others get on board. I want you to be in good shape to survive everything headed our way, and I want you to have a brilliant time doing it.

I don't want to see you drowning in debt or floating in the debris of 20 million other kids with a 2:1 in Social Science.

I worry that, too often, being young is seen as a process: Get from this year to that. Get from this school to that. Get from college to university. We give birth to actual people, but then treat them like sausages until they are at least 21, if not longer.

Being treated like a sausage is not the point of being young. Being young is the greatest adventure of all time. I loved every breathtaking minute I was doing something I shouldn't or couldn't or wasn't supposed to do.

Get on the ride, get your hands up in the air, and be as free as you can possibly be. You will never regret giving a different life a try.

The parable of Poppy

This may come across as odd, but I am about to use my own daughter as an example of how to do things. I say 'odd' because clearly I am not the greatest example of how to mother a child like my daughter. I have never been asked to be a godmother in my life. My baseline for successful parenting is that the child stays alive, and I can't stand people who brag or use their kids as a great example of anything. But ... here goes.

My middle daughter, Poppy, was supposed to be going to college to do A levels in chemistry, math, and biology. God only knows why anyone would choose these three infernal subjects that are beloved by those without an emotional bone in their body, and which require about as much empathy as an artist in isolation. But this was all part of her grand plan to become an army medic.

Now, I would love for her to become an army medic, mostly because I adore the army, believe military training should be compulsory for all at 16 years old, and would just love to see her lazy bones whipped through the Military Academy because it is so damned hard.

I went through it, and I would love to see one of my children suffer as I suffered so they can respect just how tough I am. (You could argue this statement makes me a sociopath, but mothers who clean their kids' bathrooms and bedrooms, and take their teenage crap, will understand.)

On Saturdays Poppy works as a milkmaid on a farm down at the end of our road. I know this sounds improbable and slightly pornographic, and I appreciate that 'milkmaids' conjures up the image of small waists and big tits, all milky udders and soft hands on penis-shaped teats.

But soft porn aside, she loves it, has stuck at it like a trooper, and gets herself up at 4am every Saturday to work for six hours under cows' udders to come home smelling of piss, shit and farm – which is not all that normal for a 15-year-old these days.

I look at other teenagers on Instagram, preening and posing for the camera, and wonder if there is anything going on in their pretty little heads.

The other night, we had a revelation. As her schoolteachers continue to point out, Poppy has a large brain but prefers not to use it. She is slack with her homework, doesn't revise, and frankly can't really be bothered with theory, books or discipline. She blasted through her school exams thanks to the relentlessness of her private-school teachers and Covid making things such that exams were cancelled.

Going to do A levels in highly disciplined subjects at a college where she wouldn't be obliged by strict teachers or me paying fees would be a recipe for disaster; I suspect Poppy already knew this in her heart, and I strongly suspect she had only said she would go to college because what else are you supposed to say at 15? If we go back to our sausage-processing analogy, kids get told they go from school to college.

But she loves to farm. Her heart calls her to that place, even at 4am in minus 2 degrees Celsius. It makes her feel alive. Every extra shift she gets makes her feel like she is winning, and I am super proud of her for having achieved that. I am proud of her ballsiness; I am proud of how hard she works in the cold and dark; and I am proud that she is built strong enough to lug sheep and push back against cattle.

So we sat down and ripped everything up. We ripped up the plan for A levels, discarded the military medic idea, threw away anything cautious or sensible, and applied for agricultural college, where she can farm, learn, and possibly board overnight if she chooses, in a majority-male environment where boys are men and men drive machines.

Clearly this plan has many flaws. Poppy could well end up pregnant in her first term, sod agricultural college, and end up as a homeless drunk on the streets of some festering town that time forgot. Or, worse still, Bradford.

And I will have been proven to be a catastrophic failure of a mother. I accept all these possibilities.

But it might just be that, by heading off the path at 90 degrees and following the thing she actually loves doing, her new road to becoming a little diamond will be set in motion – and how bracing that journey is going to be! For the first time in a long time, I can see her genuinely excited for her next step, and that is how all young people deserve to feel, genuinely alive to (and perhaps a little bit frightened of) their next thing.

(Full confession: I am secretly hoping she will marry a very rich farmer, build me a bespoke granny annex with uninterrupted views of hills and cows, and furnish me with warm milk and fresh eggs on a daily basis. And just maybe the odd roast dinner on a Sunday. Not that it is all about me, you understand – not at all.)

In summary, this is how to think about university:

1. The alternative to university is not 'do nothing'. Even if you firmly believe that there are no jobs, you hate your home, you can't stand living in your city for another second, or you need a change in your life, these things do not make university the right answer or the only one. But at least you know your question: what the hell am I going to do next?

2. Together with a friend who has lived a bit and a pint of some fortifying libation (ideally not cheap cider), make two columns on a page. In one, write 'University'. In the other, write every single other thing you could possibly do tomorrow. No limits, no constraints, no bad ideas, no discounting before you even write it down. Just write it down, the madder the better.

3. Try to listen to your heart and not your head. Heads trying to be terribly sensible about things are laced with restrictions

and caution. Heads are easily filled by concerned parents, sensible teachers, and worries. You need to listen to your heart. It will take you to something you love. My heart always takes to the road. Staying in one place for any length of time takes all the discipline I can muster. What does your heart tell you to do?

4. If you still feel in a muddle, get your kit sorted into one small bag, and get on the road. Get lonely enough to find yourself. It's brave, but far better than being a stupid sausage.

5. If the road feels too risky, why not take a year out and do any job you can get? A day's laboring here, a handyman job there, or be Mr. Odd Job and do anything for cash (maybe not anything – we try to keep some standards). After a year in the real world, you will wonder what on earth all those other daft lunatics thought they were gaining by spending £50,000 to get a worthless degree.

I feel certain that if you take 'doing nothing' out of the equation and force yourself to think about real alternatives to university, something on this list will be your path to making your heart sing. Find what makes you happy and keep doing it, my loves. You will never look back.

CHAPTER 5

HELP, MY FRIENDS ARE A***HOLES

Being WOKE takes many guises. Whether it's because you are a woman, want to be a woman, black, not black enough, too black, or passionate about saving the planet, any of these is enough to get a free pass to the WOKE club. In fact, the entry point has become fairly simple: You just need to hate straight white men – and the women who love them. That seems to be the starting point for all of the WOKE brigade, and perfectly sufficient and validated in their eyes to be accepted as the norm.

As a straight, white, conservative woman who loves a straight, white man, I am here to remind you why it is okay to be all of those things and how to survive the relentless encroachment of WOKEDOM on every aspect of our lives.

I would also like to remind younger readers that whites were not always the baddies. Historically, we were terrific: colonizers of an empire, bastions of military strength, and steeped in history and tradition. The Union Jack flag used to be a mark of quality. And for those who scoff – because your teachers have brainwashed you that all of these were dark deeds of extreme evil – when did you last meet a man who had found a new country and discovered a potato? Modern whites are pretty excited if they find a car parking space at the supermarket and discover the doughnuts have been reduced in aisle 4.

The WOKE brigade has played an absolute blinder at segmenting society into infinitesimally small sub-sections and then pitting them against each other to divide and disrupt. I only wish we had responded with unity and strength instead of apology and bended knee.

Black Lives Matter (BLM) is undoubtedly the most powerful movement to emerge out of WOKEDOM, capitalizing on centuries of hurt and decades of progress against racism in society. It is a regressive movement that has managed to take us back to where we were told that we hate each other based on skin color. In truth, despite flashpoints of hurt or anger, we were all muddling on rather well. I would go so far as to say that many of us had not even given any thought to color in a long time, other than to wonder why being white is the wrong answer.

I wouldn't like to be told that I can't do the same as another person because of my color, but these same discriminations exist today right under our noses; it's just the color that has changed. In the UK, if you are white, you are restricted from applying for certain jobs, cannot access certain training, and are last in line for any position or post – simply because you are not black or an ethnic minority. All of which sounds pretty racist to me.

It is also worth pointing out that white people are a minority in London, Luton, Bradford, Birmingham, and beyond – and yet they do not qualify for special treatment, because they are the 'wrong' color.

No one is allowed to say it, but it is damned annoying to see every white presenter on TV replaced by a black person, for no other reason than that this is the agenda that corporate types must now kowtow to. Ads can't possibly feature a white man and white woman who love each other and have white children; if there aren't two lesbians and a black transvestite, the ad will never make it to the screen.

The death of George Floyd, ostensibly from a fentanyl overdose and undoubtedly assisted by a police officer kneeling on his neck for eight minutes, was the starting gun that Black Lives Matter needed to propel the movement onto the global stage. Its playbook is basic, but devastatingly effective.

Here's my five-step guide, the Black Lives Matter Playbook for Dummies, to creating a global movement capable of completely screwing up race relations.

1. Call the movement something that's already true or undeniably accurate

Something like Water is Wet or People Need to Pee. (Dogs Shouldn't Be Fried Alive could also be an example, but the Chinese do this all the time and have built an entire festival around it in Yulin – something that the Left doesn't seem to have much of a problem with.)

The beautiful thing about campaigning under a bloody obvious truth is that no one can really argue with you. And the moment anyone tries to criticize your movement about anything at all – be it for looting, arson, defacing monuments, defecating in the streets, or attacking the elderly – you can simply refer to your undeniably accurate strapline: 'Are you saying Water Isn't Wet?' And, of course, it is the critics who will then appear foolish.

2. Make your movement's symbol something that works for women – and the front pages

White people love a good handshake. It involves another person, is manly yet warm, and it allows you to quickly assess who is the dominant player, like rutting stags or massive walruses fighting. However, it is not good for women of a certain age who are losing their grip on their upper arm and its skin. (My own skin's elasticity is equal to that of poorly kneaded dough, thanks to my mother, and so shaking my bingo wings when I am trying to create a good first impression is not ideal.)

BLM has nailed this: The Black Power salute involves punching a clenched fist to the sky. Not only does this work brilliantly for photos; it also offers the opportunity for even the flabbiest of bingo wings to appear active and somewhat engaged. Having such a great physical gesture will win you headlines, Instagram squares, and powerful-looking moments of stillness in the face of turmoil and disruption. The Black Power salute is, in fact, genius – and credit should be given to Adolf Hitler for inspiring the BLMers in this way.

It follows that if your movement is called, for example, People Need to Pee, then perhaps your symbol could be a simple squat, thereby engaging your thigh muscles and having you look like you are big on CrossFit or an acrid fan of the Sumo scene. I do wonder whether a picture of middle-aged protesters all looking like they are taking a shit would be all that flattering, so perhaps this element still needs work. But iconic symbols will always be iconic, so borrow one.

3. Latch onto something popular, like a tic on a dog, and steal its power

Choose your host wisely: Formula One, American football, the British Premier League – essentially anything with a mass audience that is loved unconditionally by millions. All you need to do is convince one or two of its best-loved players, drivers, or try scorers to be a part of your movement, and you have found a massive recruiting tool and PR opportunity for your campaign.

Handily for BLM, American football already had the biggest cockwomble of the lot, Colin Kaepernick, be willing to sacrifice his professional career for a far more lucrative occupation in WOKEDOM. But the Brits weren't going to be outdone: BLM in the UK recruited Lewis Hamilton, who gobbled up Black Lives Matter whole. Now he cannot open his mouth without forcing the black agenda all over the crowds that come to watch him race. Mercedes Benz even painted his car black just to reinforce the point.

How painting a car black means that Black Lives Matter is uncertain, but it is key to the movement's success not to ask awkward questions, but rather to nod along approvingly and apologize for being white. Water Is Wet might like to consider the Olympics or Wimbledon, for example – not only is water essential to athletic achievement but it underlines the irrefutable truth that Water is indeed… Wet.

In any case, latching onto these popular sports has allowed the movement to monopolize mass audiences to maximum effect. Most of these sports-loving crowds turn out to enjoy a hot dog and a beer with their families in the sunshine while watching feats of athleticism. Instead, they have blackness shoved down their throats sideways.

4. Go opposite to the norm

If the norm is up, go down. If the norm is yes, say no. If the norm is to stand, kneel. Got it?

For your movement to succeed, you can metaphorically butt up against the system by doing the opposite of what you are supposed to do. My children mastered this at an early age when any attempts by me to say 'Stop that!' resulted in their doing it more, even if that involved putting peas up their nose or my son sticking his small penis into the pencil sharpener.

BLMers have been kneeling all over the place. But soon they will grow bored of it; once everyone starts kneeling the contrast will rather lose itself and they will all just look like a bunch of numpties with no legs.

For our Water is Wet campaign, I suggest we opt for lying down. I am unclear as to how this has anything to do with water being wet, but that is not the point – what does kneeling have to do with black lives mattering? If we lie down, we beat them at their own game – they will be kneeling, and we will be lying down. To outdo us, they will have to dig trenches, and that will be both time-consuming and dirty.

5. Make agreement compulsory

With an irrefutable truth as a name (Water is Wet), a flattering gesture (a squat), mass coverage from latching onto the Olympics, and lying down at every opportunity, you are now in a great position to make agreeing with your movement compulsory.

Anyone who expresses any resistance to it, even if by accident or courtesy of an unguarded tweet, must be made to pay for it with their job, their livelihood, and even their family's safety. Any dissent must result in that individual being made unemployable as a lesson to others that no other thought is allowed, only 'agreed' thought. And the only acceptable position is to prostrate oneself to the cause. These movements operate according to standard procedures that are as predictable as they are depressingly effective.

Meanwhile, white apologists must stand by and watch statues, road names, and respect for benefactors of the past being torn down and literally and figuratively thrown in the bin, to reflect the leftist worldview. We are required to believe that history must be told differently, the past is always wrong, white is always bad, and destruction will lead to a better future.

This is brought into sharp relief by the case of Cecil Rhodes, a benefactor of Oriel College, Oxford. His donations to the college make it possible for students, including BAME (Black, Asian, and Minority Ethnic) students, to attend Oxford on a scholarship. In June 2020 Oriel College voted to remove Rhodes' statue from the outside of the college building.

The campaign group 'Rhodes Must Fall', focused on this act of destruction for years, has said it is 'hopeful' but cautious and would not be satisfied until 'the Rhodes Statue ceases to adorn the facade of Oriel College on Oxford's High Street', and that, until then, it would continue its protests over 'Imperial and colonial iconography' on university buildings. Not content with this barbarism, the college is going to launch an independent commission of inquiry into the legacy of Cecil Rhodes, which also includes scholarships at the university.

What utter madness is this? Even students who have been recipients of Cecil Rhodes' generosity have joined the campaign – the very young people who have enjoyed an education they would not otherwise have had had it not been for the money provided by him.

South African student Joshua Nott, 23, was part of a sister campaign at the University of Cape Town, where he and others attempted to tear down a statue of Cecil Rhodes on the basis that it symbolized racism and colonialism. He said that the figure was akin to a 'swastika in Jerusalem'. Yet this same student is the recipient of a £40,000 Rhodes Scholarship to study law at Oxford University. If that weren't enough, the Nott family is very wealthy and could afford to fund Joshua's course without help. Joshua's response to this is that he is just better than other people: 'If an underprivileged person could effect as much change, I would easily renounce it, but I firmly believe in myself as someone who can effect immense change.' How pompous can one over-privileged kid be?

Defending its decision to award this cretin a scholarship from the very trust he campaigned to destroy, the Rhodes Trust said, 'We pick young people of enormous ability without regard to any political affiliation… Mr. Nott has been involved in a wide range of social-change initiatives. He made this perfectly clear.'

In 2015 another anti-Rhodes activist, Ntokozo Qwabe, was

awarded the scholarship and 50,000 people petitioned for it to be taken away, but without success.

You really can't make this up. If I left a wad of cash to Oxford University in the hopes that decent patriots of the Commonwealth might receive funding and achieve a place there, I would not want it handed out to those who disagreed with my work or my income. If a statue of me had been erected (what a fabulous idea!), if any of these festering fools so much as placed a finger on my leg hair (in bronze), I would demand that any cash they had ever received in my name should be clawed back, with interest.

The simple truth is that, because Cecil Rhodes was a White Person Who Was Really Good At Stuff, he made enough cash not only to fund and feed his own lifestyle but to recognize that he wanted to use it to improve the lives of others too.

It takes a great deal of sinister manipulation to make this a bad thing. Those who are supposed to preserve his legacy are part of the self-loathing white cohort that are apologizing for both themselves and the benefactor whose legacy contributes to their salaries.

It is even more perverse that a collective of supposedly educated college sorts was so cripplingly spineless that it voted to have Rhodes's statue taken down – even if it subsequently recanted – because that is the 'right opinion' and the only one that guarantees job tenure in the face of the baying mob.

This is the Black Lives Matter playbook. It is a template, used over and over, by all of WOKEDOM. Only the way that the group identifies itself changes, whether by gender, sexuality, politics, or environmentalist tendencies.

We are groomed into conforming from an early age at school, programmed to believe that it is safer to be on the side of the mob, and taught through example that the only way to hold onto things we value in our lives (job, home, safety) is to keep our heads down and comply.

It takes a brave warrior to take on WOKEDOM. We need to build individuals strong enough to stand alone and stronger still to face down the WOKE mob. Taking a knee to stupidity is to genuflect to assholes. Stand up, look up, and see through this madness.

CHAPTER 6

HELP, I'M SINGLE

Girl, I hear you.

I can't begin to tell you the outrage I feel when I meet vivacious and lovable women and am just complimenting them on their hair or teeth or boobs (usually all three) and telling them how great they look when they ask me why they are still single, or why men never say those things to them.

They are so sick of being single, so done with the misery of dating; they just desperately want to find Mr. Right and be married and settled down. Single women are exhausted by the effort of it all.

If you are one of them, you are not alone. It is of absolutely zero comfort to know that you are many – but it is equally annoying when it feels like everyone else is married or having babies, with the perfect ring, the perfect husband, and the perfect house.

I am also here to tell you it's not you.

And I don't mean that in the 'it's not you, it's me' sense; I mean it in the 'the world changed, the internet happened, and dickheads at Google screwed it all up for you' sense.

You didn't change or get less lovely; the world got less good at letting lovely people find each other.

Most brilliant women I meet don't want a man so they can quit working, put their feet up and take it easy. Nor do they want it because it's the traditional way and what women are supposed to do. Women simply want a life partner with whom to share their happy days and sad days. It's the most honest reason for wanting to get married – wanting to have someone who is completely yours to share your life with and to be there for in return. I totally get it.

And I see the misery being endured by so many trying to do the dating thing, particularly in America – more specifically, Florida – where the whole scene feels altogether more cruel.

I feel guilty, too, because I am married and have been so twice. I have a waitlist for husband number three, yet I know that I am a royal pain in the ass – and, in reality, these men would run a mile if they actually knew me. I snore, I rarely get a pedicure, and I am demanding and impatient.

These beautiful single women I know would make far nicer wives than I will ever manage to be, I am certain of it, but somehow it's easier to attract a man when you have a man. A bit like mussels (as in the seafood) on the pier, I guess – once one little shellfish sees another, it latches on because this must be a good place to hang out. If there are no other shellfish, maybe this pier is a flipping mad woman with cats (if you follow my line of thought).

It's a bit like women who can't seem to get pregnant or have children. Typically they are the sort of women who would make the greatest parent in the world, and yet dodgy mums like me only have to sniff sperm at a thousand paces and we are up the duff.

If it isn't already hugely overstated in every single chapter in this book, I love men. I prefer them to women. I love real men's strength and roughness; I particularly love men in work overalls and steel-toe-capped boots. And unlike my hardcore lesbian allies, I do not think men are to blame for everything – in fact, I find most of them, outside of soy boys, simps, and short malcontents, to be fabulous.

Men tend to be less judgy than women, less weirdly competitive about the stuff that doesn't matter, and less interested in stirring up drama just so they can be part of it. If you tell a man you don't want to talk about it, they understand what you mean and don't talk about it. Women will pick at it like a festering sore until you bleed.

I believe straight women are supposed to have one special man in their life. But if you are currently single and can't find him no matter how hard you try, we can agree it is not fair, and there is no reason on God's green earth why you are single, no explanation that makes sense.

Take my friend from California, 'Angel'. She has the most amazing thick hair. I can't take my eyes off it when I am with her; it feels like it is life cascading out of her heart onto her shoulders, while my own is thinner than a cheap white wine. Not only is she bright, bubbly and curvy, but she is intelligent, fun, and has a wicked laugh and a perfect smile to go with it. At forty-something she is my definition of perfect – whatever 'perfect' means.

'Perfect' probably means different things to different men. If I were a man, I would be attached to her like – well, like a mussel to a pier.

She is a successful teacher, owns her own house, and is a delight to be around. Unlike my good self, she has not had a series of children with different men, been fired from every job she's ever had, or been caught naked in a field. Nor does she look like Princess Anne or Boris Becker in a certain light.

And yet she is single.

But her Mr. Perfect must be out there because I firmly believe there is someone out there for all of us – and that 'someone' can, on occasion, change.

My girlfriends ask me, 'Where are all the men? Where is my Mr. Right?' And I tell them I just don't get it. It makes me sad because, given that their person (and alternative options) is out there, it must be that they just haven't been able to find him as easily as they might have in the past.

Somewhere along the line, something went really badly wrong with dating, particularly in America. I am pretty sure that the culprit in all of this is the internet.

In the glory days of my youth, my friends and I went out on the weekend, typically hooked up with someone, or 'many ones', and if any of those blessed creatures wanted to see us again, they would have to find us the next weekend, ring us on an actual phone, or get a message to us via our mates that they wanted to take us out for a drink or a walk – or, in the case of me and Jimmy, a sneaky snog by the sports field.

I remember running down the alleyway behind our school in my freaky convent girl uniform for this very purpose; it is seared into my memory. It was a Great Awakening of my very own – that even in the middle of a mundane life as a convent school kid being taught by joyless nuns, you could make a dash for freedom and have your face snogged off in the lunch break by a boy from the dodgy comprehensive school up the road. Jimmy smelt of cigarettes and bad things; and he was simply terrific.

Growing up in the 80s everything was in person and personal. The only way you could really get to know someone, or they you, was in person. Phone calls meant something, and hours spent talking on the line to a new boyfriend, with neither of you wanting to put the phone down first, were the foundation of some of my longest relationships in my early years. Those old enough to join in with me here will remember the delight of having a single house phone attached to the wall by a curly cable, and having to sneak into the coat room with the thing to try and get some privacy from parents and prying ears.

Others tell me about the 'party line', a single telephone line shared by four or six neighbors, where you had to wait your turn and could listen in to others' conversations if you were that way inclined. Or sufficiently perverted.

My father would shout, 'Get off the phone!' and eventually, grudgingly, I would, mortified that the object of my affections had heard my father's voice and that, as a fully independent 14-year-old, I had been told what to do.

Even now, when I am on the road my husband and I talk by phone without video because we both know that we listen better and our conversation is more meaningful. Why do people have to see each other when they speak on the phone these days? Why do people feel the need to hold their phone at arm's length and shout at the other person, like everyone wants to hear their damned conversations? Why do you need to see the person you are talking to?

Women like me were lucky to find husbands in a time before the invasion of the internet into the dating scene. The internet invasion changed everything, and not just in obvious ways such as online dating. It took away the personal: The phone calls dialed from a landline, where you really had to commit to the call and the time to make it; the normalcy of speaking to a man in a bar without effectively creating an appointment to do that via an app; and the expectation of going out and being attracted to someone – and that being the reason to have a conversation in that moment. The internet took away the permission for all the things that made magic stuff happen. And all the while, it told us we were 'more connected than at any time in history'.

It lied.

I look at what women now endure in the age of internet dating, and it truly sucks – harder than a man eating ribs with no teeth. The only thing suckier than internet dating is the competitive engagement scene in New York City, where engagement proposals are restaged for professional photographers and cinematographers so that the power couple of a group can create mind-blowing content for social media. They are happy and successful, goddamn it, and you are going to know about it.

The size of the ring is directly proportional to the level of assholery involved in this process. And daddy is more than happy to pay for it to make sure his daughter gets what she wants.

I've known many a fiancée's father sling the new boy the cash for the diamond of her choosing. I spoke to a woman who did exactly this: She told her new husband to go get the cash from her father because that was the ring she wanted and that was the ring she was going to have. She was not going to be made to look less successful in front of her friends because her future husband could not afford the rock of her choice.

This is grim, and I hope my children have no part in this circus. I'd rather they had a band made of string or grass. Or no ring at all. If happiness is dependent on others seeing it, or being jealous of it, is it really true happiness at all?

But I hear you; these are things that we already know. And where's the help in that? This book is supposed to be giving HELP, not telling us shit we already know that we already feel bad about.

It's coming, I promise.

It cannot be that the men who women want have ceased to exist; they must still be out there, in the same way that my ex-boyfriends and husbands are out there, all marvelous in their own way. These men are still out there swimming in the sea, like the 'plenty more fish' that unhelpful aunties tell you to go find. I meet these fish all the time – at conferences, at bars and in stores. There are loads of men out there looking for a lady to love.

But we aren't catching each other like we used to, with magic, stolen glances, snogs on the dance floor, or too much Bacardi and Coke. In times before, we reeled in our catch by meeting again in daylight, or drinking again, or dancing again after talking on the phone. Or, in my case, kissing them again. (I remain an expert kisser of men.)

It mattered, too, how you treated that new girl or guy because they were real to you; they were a real person with a personality and a family, and these moments together were very real as well. Your new man had all of your attention.

We didn't endlessly message or text because we couldn't. But now texting or messaging is the only acceptable way that couples connect or date – an actual phone call would be weird at best, way too intimate for most; what on earth would you talk about? Actually connecting meaningfully has come to mean being needy or clingy in some way.

These days, women who have dangled off the end of a man's cock in a hotel room are not able to pick up the phone and speak to that same man's ear. Is that not the cruelest twist of all?

Dating has become some hideous sushi bar where men and women revolve around on an endlessly moving conveyor belt and the diner plucks off the dish they like the look of, has a nibble or two, and then puts it back if they change their mind. Swiping, liking, scrolling, endless movements that don't bring men and women together so much as reduce people to the sum of their parts: face, boobs, location. Or, on the gay scene, dick, biceps, face; I am reliably told by my gay mates that is the order of priority and I am not at liberty to question this rationale even if I wanted to, although, to be fair, speaking as a straight woman, they are on to something.

With endless choice, organized by age, body parts, and location, it makes sense to cast your net wide online. You have an endless array of options and possibilities, so why not go for all of them? And, if Sarah falls through, there is always Rebecca to fall back on or another woman or man to give you the compliment you need that night … by text message … in an app. A crumb that makes you feel better about yourself for an instant, fleeting and empty, disappearing just as fast as it came.

And I know it makes you feel worse, not better, knowing that little message from 'him' was a boost, checking your phone to see if he messages again, wondering why he doesn't, persecuting yourself into holding out until he replies so you can reply again. What a massive mind overload all of this is. We are truly messing with ourselves.

It is rough, really rough. I see the way that boys are changing and some men too, wanting all of the fun bits without commitment or the messiness of meaningful contact. Many of them trust me like a man, or at least see me as one. And so I get to see the way they operate firsthand.

Men confide in me like they would in another man. I am guessing this is partly because they know I am not there for the taking, and partly because I seem manly in my ways. I am a straight talker so they tell me the stuff they know other women would not want to hear.

It would be wrong to tiptoe past the fact that there is a real stigma attached to women who are still single at 40, so we may as well get it out in the open and deal with it straight, repeating it more or less word for word from the men I have heard it from:

'Look, you gotta take it as a warning light. Not married? Still single? No kids at 40? There's gotta be something going on there, right? That's an express ticket to walking up the aisle and being caught with babies you never wanted but you've gotta pay for, right there. I mean, if no other man has gone there, something's up. It's either cats or kids.'

Men tell me if they meet someone who is single at 40, never married, and childless, she must have a screw lose. We know this rule does not apply to men, only to women, but no one really talks honestly about it. And no man will ever admit to thinking like this to a regular woman because he doesn't want to sound like a jerk.

There is also pure fear in most men (also single or looking for a woman to make them feel good about themselves) that their life of sport, freedom, and sex with pretty ladies is going to be curtailed by dating a woman who is desperate to settle down and have kids.

For them, it's an unfathomable conundrum: 'Why won't women just give me a blow job, have sex with me, say nice things to me, see me when I want them to, and otherwise leave me alone? Why do they have to be so needy?'

They look at me in disbelief when I tell them that women want them to care. Women want this to be more than a transaction. Women want to believe this is all going somewhere – and that isn't up the aisle, it's just into a meaningful relationship with someone who cares.

Online dating has made boys feel that this soulless sexing is the new normal, and this is reinforced with every new hookup they have and every new woman they sleep with in exchange for no commitment at all. In many ways, we have brought this on ourselves.

Worse still, new men aren't men at all. We have plunged down a dark ravine in which purebred heterosexuals have become metrosexuals, who have become soys and small asexual nothings with a sperm count lower than Caster Semenya (the female track star with internal testes and a wife). None of this has anything to do with being straight or gay; it's just a very long way from the capable-man type that yearns for a lovely-wife type with whom to settle down and have kids.

I get that men and women meet just for sex and separate straight afterwards on the understanding that's all the arrangement ever was. And I respect anyone who is into this and gets what they really need out of it.

I know married men and women who have affairs running alongside their marriage and are adamant that the reason they are still happily married is because of the outlet the third person in the marriage gives them.

Feminists argue casual sex is empowering – it is women using their bodies and getting what they want and need for themselves.

But I suspect this is actually an illusion. Far from being empowering, it may actually be more like self-harm. For the briefest of moments, perhaps, that man tells you what you want to hear, or makes you feel attractive or important to him. But if there is nothing more than the physical, what are you really getting back in return?

Each time, you are giving away a precious piece of yourself that detracts from the sum of your parts; it takes some of your light, and you have to regenerate that power to shine as brightly as before.

I am not saying don't have sex and lots of it. I am not saying don't have sex with strangers or men you see repeatedly for sex but nothing else. I am just asking you to be honest with yourself – brutally honest – about what you are really getting out of it.

Are you really getting what you want?

If the answer is yes, then go you. If the outward answer is yes but in your heart it's a no, then we are getting somewhere.

Perhaps you do want the full marriage/happy husband/ babies thing and, at 40, cannot afford to be messing around. Lovely women who are inexplicably still single are at the point where they feel they are better off just cutting to the chase. Perhaps this is you?

You want to know: What's the point of pretending to be nonchalant and nonplussed when, behind the facade, your body clock is chiming like a chuffing church bell at a funeral and you want an Insta-perfect wedding dress and a baby on the way within six months of being sat at this very bar? What's the point of pretending to be Miss Casual and Miss Super Cool when you aren't?

I think this is both smart and honest. But I would argue this is also the perfect rationale for deleting online dating apps, which are designed for the very things you don't want: disposable moments. I also wonder about the wisdom of discrediting everything that might be fun due to your laser focus on finding a husband.

Relationship experts describe the situation of a woman knowing she wants something more meaningful than a quick 'rogering' and an Uber ride home as the Amazon Prime complex; the woman wants to check off a few boxes and have the perfect candidate arrive at her mailbox in 48 hours. Their distinctly useless advice is to be patient, stay positive, and think of frustration like a blizzard – it will do nothing but delay the delivery.

This is trite crap. You can't just put impatience in a cupboard and lock it away. Women have an internal clock and it ticks, no matter how much we may try to override it. Imagining that your frustration is a blizzard isn't all that helpful when you are in your pajamas crying into your lasagna for a man because you are lonely. Plus, it's hardly an Amazon Prime complex when you have been shopping for a decent man for the best part of 40 years – that's a lot of time spent browsing to leave the store empty-handed.

I also remind women that these relationship experts they listen to are as needy as the next woman and are typically single themselves, but for good reasons. They're like the women who work in Human Resources – they feed off and gossip about your pain as a way of making themselves feel better about their own lives. Privately, they live alone with cats and a vibrator for company – which is not to be mocked; everyone should try it. But these private lives betray the fact they are not experts on anything but cats and vibrators.

Set against this new reality faced by single women, particularly women nearer to 50 than 20, I have a five-point plan for anyone seeking a man. It is not subtle or pretty, but I share it as someone who is your greatest cheerleader in your search for love.

1. Don't look for a husband

Neither of my husbands thus far has been the result of looking for one, although that sentence may not inspire oodles of confidence if you are looking to settle down and can't stand the thought of divorce.

I also understand that, if you have failed to find yourself a single husband just yet, my having had two already is both annoying and greedy. What can I say? I can't lie and I can't change my past. Unbeknownst to me, I was also sharing my first husband with another woman (probably many more), so I am less greedy than it seems.

I ended up with my first husband after I saw him looking utterly shattered in the office at the end of a very long day and asked how he was doing; that was enough, apparently. Six months later, we had both given up everything (homes, partners, children (his)), moved to New York, and started a new life.

When I homed in on my current husband, Lovely Mark, I was only really looking for a passionate partner. I wanted him and I was determined he would be mine. But he turned out to be too lovely to leave me, and the poor man has been trapped by my unlikely charms for over a decade. He is my person and I will never have another husband in this life.

But I totally get that it is different if you are looking for a father for your future baby. It is all very well to say 'don't go out looking for a husband' when you are under biological time pressure and you need a husband and a baby father before your eggs become hardboiled and your fertility window slams shut like a frigging fire door.

But going out and looking for a husband/baby daddy is like security screening at an airport, except that no one gets through.

Every man you set eyes on has to pass a checklist of criteria before he gets to have a conversation with you. What's the point of chatting with the shorter, balding guy at the bar when you know you couldn't possibly be married to someone like that? Worse still, imagine the kind of baby he might produce!

I am not saying you should be grateful for anything. You should not lower your expectations; nor should you pretend to be interested in a man who doesn't make you smile or laugh. But not every meeting can be a recruitment process for a husband or suitable sperm. What does suitable sperm even look like?

I believe the very best things happen in life when we throw ourselves to the wind. Time with men should be like this too – even if he is already your husband. What about trying to meet someone to have fun with? If you had someone nice to go with, what would be your favorite thing, and how could you make it lovely for both of you? On my list are nights away at nice hotels, quiet walks somewhere new, pub lunches, and surfing on the coast. All pretty harmless stuff.

The next thing you do with someone should just be for harmless fun. Maybe he won't be the one. But if he can make you laugh and stop thinking about the days beyond today, you might just giggle your way into a whole new relationship.

2. Take a break from online dating

Delete all the dating apps on your phone and give yourself some time away from it. This doesn't have to be forever; it's not like you are committing to being a vegan and vowing that meat will never pass your lips again even though you are secretly yearning for bacon every weekend. But I think it is really important to reclaim the space in your life that is currently constipated by dating apps and swiping through photos or endlessly text-messaging men you haven't met or aren't going to meet anytime soon. Do you really need to send or receive a nod or a wink or some other meaningless emoji?

Dating apps feel like a trap, just as addictive as any social media, giving you a serotonin flush when you receive flirty messages or compliments from men you have liked or matched with, but not really getting anywhere in terms of meeting someone with whom you'd love to have a real relationship.

Plenty of men will be reading this, too, and feeling these exact same things about women.

Dating apps seem to benefit complete jerks the most, or at least those with the most issues. And in a man's case, the ease with which they can pick up another woman is the same ease with which they can drop them back down: 'It was only an online thing, so whatever.'

I have heard stories of women waiting to meet a date who either doesn't show or ghosts them after a week or so. I can only imagine the effort it takes to hold your pride together but I do know it would take courage and hurt like hell.

Someone not showing up when you made yourself look nice and made the effort to go out and meet them is nasty, plain nasty. It makes me want to get a baseball bat and come charging to your side. You deserve better than that. Save yourself the bloodied nose.

3. Go to a place where there are real men

There is little point sitting in the same little town in the same state thinking your luck will change and Mr. Right will suddenly show up unexpectedly at your local restaurant or wine bar.

It is time to take yourself to a state where heterosexual man can be seen and admired in the wild. Remember, you are going on safari, and the idea is to watch the animals and talk to them. You are not going husband-hunting or to get a trophy husband to take home and pin to your wall (although that's good if it happens). Rather, you are there to be reminded of what it feels like to be in a bar surrounded by good men. Bikers gravitate to each other's testosterone; if you can hear the 'thrub thrub thrub' of a bike engine or smell petrol, you are probably getting warmer. I do this often, and it is therapy for my soul.

This advice comes with a warning. The Covid age and the tech twats from California have ushered in the age of the digital nomad whereby if you are working from home then your home can be anywhere – and, as a digital nomad, you might as well be somewhere warm and sunny, like Antigua, as opposed to languishing in Minnesota and freezing your tits off.

So beware the road. Anyone who describes himself as a digital nomad is a complete asshole with the testosterone levels of Ryan Seacrest. Do not go to a place frequented by digital nomads – Tulum, Mexico is a good example. You are more likely to find a vegan soy boy than the man you need in your life.

4. Don't try to be the person you think they are looking for

I am watching this happen in front of my very eyes this week in Mexico. It is Spring Break and it has been soul-destroying to watch utterly beautiful young girls moon about after boys who should be thanking their lucky stars these girls are even talking to them. One guy with floppy hair seems to be attracting at least two or three girls way above his pay-grade.

It angers me as a mother and woman to watch these girls be so amenable. The boys get to be brash, obnoxious asss, and the girls titter along supportively behind them like disposable appendages to frat boys and their enormous egos.

How has this happened? Why has it manifested itself? Perhaps it is an American thing, but I suspect the girls just want to be seen with those boys and are prepared to be treated pretty poorly just to be in the running.

I heard one particular little shit shouting at a girl over breakfast that just because he woke up in the bed of a beautiful girl didn't mean they did anything … and just as an FYI, not all guys are after sex all of the time; maybe sometimes they just want to hang out with beautiful women and sleep with them in their bed.

And then he stalked off to the men's room with his buddy to cool down.

'Just as an FYI' – who says that in real life, at 20? To a lovely girl! At breakfast! The utter cretin. It took a great deal of self-restraint on my part not to march over to his table, pick him up by his ear and give him an FYI of my own creation. More upsettingly, the girl just sat there and took it.

This is not about Spring Breakers per se; it is applicable to us at any age. We have all been that girl. We have all been made to feel we are the ones in the wrong or being unreasonable when we were talking perfect sense or asking the right questions.

I have pretended to be asleep in bed while my husband went outside in the car to ring his mistress, and been perfectly pleasant on his return. None of us are immune from being degraded to the point of insanity.

If you find yourself behaving in a way that you would be unable to explain to your closest friend, get out. There is no rationale. There is no justification. Your relationship will not be okay in the end; you just need to bring the end closer.

Trying to be the thing you think he wants is exhausting. You are basically playing chess two moves ahead, trying to work out what he will want to do the move after next and be ready to make it happen for him.

Not only is that a lot of head space you are taking up, but you are bound to lose. You're not going to be able to keep that act up for long, even if it does get you down the aisle, because, in truth, your end goal isn't actually getting married but rather to be happy – and that comes with your laughter lines, your wrinkles, the weird mole on your lip, the slightly odd hair line, your varicose veins, and your dodgy nipple hair (who, me?). If they can't handle that, they aren't the one for you. Hiding who you really are isn't going to improve matters.

That said, it is not necessary to display all those things on your first date or even on your second. But the principle is that you are in this to find shared happiness, not just his.

When I was getting rid of an old sofa from my home, I advertised it online as a truly awful sofa, stained and ugly, but still functioning as one. Surprisingly, I was beating potential buyers off with a stick. There was something in the honesty of the thing that made people laugh, made them feel comfortable, and made them want to own this monstrosity. I think it was the certainty that they weren't going to be ripped off or turn up to find something that didn't look like it did in the pictures that I had posted online. It was honest.

Women over 40 are not like my ugly sofa, and you should not apply this sofa principle directly. But I do think some brutal honesty is an endearing quality. I suppose it is the same as my girlfriends who are upfront and honest with a man that they want to get married and have kids and aren't really into just having oodles of casual sex and self-loathing.

When men offer me sex online or ask if they can take me out, I warn them that I am a real pain in the ass and not that attractive in person – and, like bees on a flower, they can't get enough of that stuff.

Good men are tired of all of the pretense too. Relationship gurus would call it 'embracing your baggage'. I call it 'your best bits'. Go show 'em off to anyone who will take a look.

5. Remember you are fantastic

You know that moment when you catch your own reflection in a shop window or a glass, and your first thought is, 'Christ on a bike! What the hell do I look like?!' We do a lot of that in life – judging ourselves harshly from reflection, whether these are photos, looking in a mirror, or the comments of others that we misread, misinterpreted, or read a tone into that simply wasn't there when the message was written.

If you look at a picture, do you pick out the great bits about yourself? No, you pick out the things you worry about (your hairline, spots, chins, whatever). And if you look at a group picture with family or friends, do you look at the whole moment or zoom in on yourself to see how bad you look?

This has to stop. You have to know you are fantastic and believe it. Go back to a recent photo you like and write down all the things that are great about you, or what the photo actually captured. The photo captured a moment – what was that all about? I doubt it has anything to do with how you look.

Stop making a stick out of nothing and beating yourself about the head with it! Life is tough enough without you being your worst critic. Leave that to someone else.

In your own heart you know who you are. I know that I am kind and want the very best for a stranger in the street; if they fell or were hurt, I would run and try to save them. And that's honestly enough for me, to know that I am good – no matter how crappy my hair looks or how weird the varicose vein on my shin looks (it is very weird).

But you, you are fantastic. Forget finding a husband. Find 'happy' instead.

CHAPTER 7

HELP, I'M HAVING A BABY

'OOOOoooooofff! That's going to sting a bit!'

This is my absolutely favorite expression to blurt out to pregnant mums who have a massive bump and look like they are expecting triplets.

I like to make that sucking-in 'sooouuu' noise you make through your teeth when something is really going to hurt, while staring directly at their bump and vaginal region with a pained expression. It's a great way to break the ice and never ceases to make me laugh.

If you are pregnant right now, you might not see the funny side – you might argue it's a touch insensitive. But I think strangers making weird cooing noises and trying to touch your belly as if this baby were some dove from above is way more strange.

Anyone who thinks it is okay to start rubbing the belly of a stranger – sticky -outie bellybutton and all – needs to be locked up. I am reminded of the men who ask me to send pictures of the soles of my feet (it's a fetish thing). When I was really preggers, one woman asked me straight out, 'Can I touch it?' and I swear I hadn't the first clue what she was talking about.

Touch what? Until I realized she meant my actual belly skin.

What's so funny about pregnancy is that people are so damned British about it – even if they are American. It's a topic no one wants to address frankly or as bluntly as a pregnant person needs.

It's particularly true of conservatives or religious types in America, who choose to pretend in public that babies are a gift from God and delivered by storks. I get that many people see children as a gift from God; I am not taking issue with anyone's beliefs. But we have to be a bit honest and acknowledge that baby got put there by doing the nasty.

For those who have been trying for a baby for years and years, getting pregnant is usually the result of endurance and applying the kind of discipline to sex you would hope your small child would apply to doing their teeth, daily if not twice daily – and occasionally in the middle of the day as well, if you are feeling good.

In my mum's day, expectant mothers were supposed to dress in huge swathes of fabric, effectively king-sized bedsheets, usually with a nautical theme – a sort of sailor's smock dress. Anything to avoid the obvious 'bump put there by a penis' conversation in church.

Even now, expectant mothers spend hours privately padding and elasticizing their way through the nine months so that nothing drops off or leaks without their noticing it. I am not saying you want to slosh your way down the road in a puddle of ooze, milk, and other fluids, but I am saying it's damned effort.

Instagram can make you feel like pregnancy is one glorious photo shoot of bikinis, cradling bumps, and delighted-looking husbands. It is not. It is utterly mad. If this is you right now and you are feeling fat, bloated, and have ankles that look like elephant legs, you are not alone. You are normal. And 'normal' does not expect to carry about a nine-pound living thing without some unpleasant consequences.

When I was having my babies, the idea was to appear to be wearing regular clothes despite having a waistline eighteen sizes bigger than normal dangling dangerously over where your front bottom used to be. The idea was to look like a regular woman in jeans and a top, despite the fact your top now had no discernible endpoint and your bottom was the size of a bus.

It is a very weird day in your young life when you look down and realize you can no longer see your own foof (front bottom). I am guessing fat people get kind of used to it but, as a skinny bird, I can tell you it is most odd.

More odd is the effort of putting on shoes or trying to bend over to pull up a pair of pants. It is not until you don't have a waist that you realize what a useful thing it is.

This weird Britishness extends to maternity classes, too. If you think signing up for maternity classes will be a good use of your time, I have to advise you otherwise.

This is the definition of prenatal classes, also called birth and parenting classes: to help you and your partner get ready for labor, birth, breastfeeding, and caring for a newborn baby. Most people say going to classes helps them to feel more confident as the birth approaches.

This is a complete lie.

Even the woman running the damned thing wants to avoid saying the thing that needs to be said: that massive watermelon you are carrying inside of you has got to get out of a hole the size of a polo mint.

The big thing/small hole becomes the elephant in the room (and by that I don't mean you). I mean, it's a bloody obvious fact that a watermelon won't easily squeeze out of an aperture of the size that can normally only extend to a family-sized salami – and that usually only after a few glasses of wine and a nice meal.

Fear not. I am here to HELP!

This is the honest prenatal class that you need. Everything you need to know about giving birth is here in this chapter. If you don't want to hear all of this, or your unhelpful mother-in-law has bought you this book out of spite, or you are eight-months pregnant and very emotional, then maybe just look away now.

But if you are scared, slightly concerned, or just needing a friend who doesn't sugarcoat stuff, here it is.

Three simple truths

The truth you should be told is – of course it bloody well hurts. Three important facts need stating:

1. In order for the baby-sized thing sitting on top of your pubic bones to get out of that calcium-reinforced fortress above your vagina, your pubic bones need to spread themselves wider than a lock on a longboat canal.

2. To push something with a head the size of – well, a baby's head – out of that tube you were a bit squeamish about inserting a Tampax Mini into, is going to feel like having a small calf pulled out of your innards with clamps and a welly boot pushed hard up against your ass.

3. Sometimes your bits aren't going to stretch enough, in which case nurses at the business end of things will make a little cut to help get the baby out. But please don't worry about this. In my experience, your bits are way more stretchy than you give them credit for, and if you prepare yourself to take the pain, your bits will give you that extra few millimeters you need.

Managing pain

Nurses at birthing classes will talk to you about controlling 'discomfort' with birthing pools, Tens machines, or Spotify playlists of soothing music.

Frankly, this is all complete bollocks. There is nothing you feel less like doing when your baby is splitting your hips in half and apparently threatening to shatter your spine than getting into a piss-warm public bath and listening to Enya.

I remember looking at the sinister pool in my maternity room and wondering if anyone had cleaned it properly after the last woman had exploded into it. It made me more determined than ever not to leave my safe doggy position on my birthing trolley.

When you are thinking about giving birth, I wouldn't try to imagine yourself lying gracefully on your back with perfect hair against your pillow. I wouldn't overthink your outfit or your underwear, either. Imagine yourself after a particularly painful exercise – sweating like a fat bird on a cross trainer, hair slapped wet across your head, ass in the air, and face biting the pillow. That's more the look you want to be prepared for.

While your underwear really isn't going to matter one iota,

your pubic hair is. I suggest getting rid of all of it. Whatever is about to happen to your undercarriage is not going to be made any easier to clean up and repair with half a bush sprouting out of your upper thigh.

Be a pain receiver

The best birthing plan is to be completely ready for pain, to be open to everything – including swearing, too much gassed air, and shitting yourself. All these things are perfectly acceptable. Your job right now is to turn yourself into a pain receiver – that is, set your brain and body to 'ready', like a receiver in American football preparing to receive the ball. Be prepared to receive pain; tell yourself this is going to hurt a bit; tell yourself you are a tough old bird, other women can do this and you are stronger than most. Tell yourself you can do this. Say it over and over. You can even imagine the stance you would take against pain, refusing to be pushed over by it or felled – like the stance you might take if a child were running at you to jump into your arms. You are braced. And you are ready.

It's just like the James Bond movie Casino Royale when the baddie cuts the bottom out of a chair, makes Bond sit on the frame, and then repeatedly swings a knotted rope into Daniel Craig's dangling balls. Who among us hasn't wished to be present for at least some of that scene? That's what childbirth is like; I think of it every time I watch that scene. I strongly recommend you find that film scene right now and watch it yourself.

Your challenge is to make like Daniel Craig and every time you are crucified by labor pains (or, in Bond's case, swatted in the gonads), you yell, 'Yes, yes, yes!' or 'Come on!' or something similar – as if you are challenging the pain to try harder to beat you. Why? Because you are a pain receiver, and you have got this!

If I am really cutting the cr*p here and being straight with you, my advice – which you should discard in an instant if it suits you to – is to try and take as much pain as you can.

I know I am a bit freaky like that, and I have built a reputation of being tough. But in my heart I can't help but feel planned C-sections are not the way to go.

Of course, this is your decision and, of course, you can do what you bloody well like. And yes, you miss out on a lot of agony. But you also miss out on being there for every damned awful minute of it. And I, even now, if given the choice again, wouldn't opt to miss out on actually making it through the pain.

Women are amazing, and we are designed to get this baby out; we are designed to do this mad thing, and the less someone else has to fiddle with your bits, your back, or your belly in the process, the better I think it seems to be.

My Mexican friends would call this antiquated. The wealthy middle class believes that pushing out a baby is a sign of being poor, and no member of decent society would countenance such a thing. New Yorkers, the same.

Which probably explains why you will typically find me in dive bars and the poorer parts of town hanging out with my kind of people, the kind of people who are not too posh to push. And I say all this from a place of kindness.

I feel the same way about epidurals. If you can't feel your own legs, how the hell are you supposed to push a baby out? You need to be putting your weight behind that thing to pop it out into the open. My own sister endured her personal nightmare after an epidural, and it is the reason why she only has one child; she would never go through again what she went through then.

In no way am I trying to be one of those weird people who make you feel bad for whatever decision you make. It is yours, and you own it.

I am trying to be your cheerleader-in-chief. I am saying, 'Do it, bird, if you can.' Do it. I have faith that every woman can go through this thing if she locks her jawbone to 'invincible' and if nature works as it should.

Whatever happens, you will do it your way. Whatever is the right answer for you is the right thing.

One thing I promise you – and on this you have my word: If you can yell, spit, sweat, or shit your way through the pain, eventually your baby will come out. Childbirth will end. It will be over. Every push is one push less.

And, somewhat shocked but relieved, you will be amazed at what you just endured, and have newfound admiration for mothers who have more than one child.

The aftermath

No one ever talks about this bit. I would have been grateful for this chapter before I went into labor, and I want to level with you so you are more prepared for it than I was. My editor says this section is a step too far; he is probably right.

I grew up in a Methodist home with a mother who was too embarrassed to discuss the subject of periods – or, indeed, any other personal matter that a girl at 14 really could have used a mother's help with.

One day she surreptitiously left a book about periods by my bedside and walked out. I don't recall her ever buying pads for me or any of the things girls need to deal with periods, either; she was simply too embarrassed by the whole thing and preferred to pretend it just wasn't happening. 'Bizarre' doesn't even come close to being the right word for it, and when I look back, it makes me kind of sad. I am sad that I never had someone at home who I could talk to about any of this stuff, and sad that I went through it alone.

On a more positive note, my mother's inability to talk about things that girls need to know has had the benefit of making me very open indeed about everything with my girls, and I am so happy for that. My girls might say I have taken things a bit far in the other direction, given I happily prance about the house naked and discuss pretty much anything in front of them. But they know without question if they have a problem, they can tell me and I will fix it. And if it is personal problem, they can tell me and we will fix it.

In a way, I think my mum's silence on all these things has taught me to be a different mum, and that's been a kind of resolution in and of itself.

But I have digressed. What I want to warn you about is the bit after.

You've got a baby; maybe you've told your mum or dad; everyone is crying and super-excited and coming in to see the baby in the morning; and you are just about recovering from the shock of what just went on. And what just went on was nothing like what anyone said it would be like – apart from me.

But it was the aftermath that really got me.

After your baby is delivered, you get to have a shower, which is moderately terrifying in itself because you know what just happened and you are unsure of which bits of you are still intact. You fear that if someone held up a mirror to your foof, it would be like a particularly gory scene from the film Good Morning Vietnam.

As I waddled out of the shower like John Wayne with hemorrhoids, I was horrified to discover that most of the blood that used to be inside of me was now making a bid for freedom. Maybe people who have heavy periods are used to this sort of thing but, frankly, I have seen less blood in a slaughterhouse.

I was somehow marooned in the shower in my own murder scene. I stood there wondering if I would eventually pass out or whether I could make it to dry land and some kind of industrial absorbent padding.

Don't do what I did! Don't be unprepared and act surprised when you are hemorrhaging like an Ebola victim in the heat. Be ready. Plan this stuff out in advance.

Plan for the aftermath

Have your granny knickers in a size 40 (ideally in black) ready on a nearby chair in the shower. Have the biggest sanitary towel in human history already locked on your pregnancy knickers, and have them fully loaded, like nachos, but with pants.

Have a pair of black/navy sweatpants (or 'tracksuit bottoms' in UK parlance) ready to layer on top. And have a spare sanitary towel ready – something the size of the fourth runway at Heathrow Airport should do it. This way, you can shove the spare runway towel between your legs as you exit the shower and dry off. And then, when you are ready, you can gingerly pull on your mighty knickers (preloaded) and swap out the shower runway towel, and voila! You are no longer marooned in your own blood.

This might make the more delicate reader want to vomit, but I seriously wish I'd had someone tell me all of this before I faced my shower slaughter scene alone. I had to eat two Mars bars and sip a strong coffee alone in my hospital chair before I was able to speak again. Then I freaked myself out by looking over into the plastic cot next to my bed and seeing a baby in it – and realizing that the baby in it was mine.

Sometimes, life really does come at you fast.

My thoughts on other mums

I should place a caveat here. It is clear from my oversharing of everything that I am not a perfect mother. In fact, I suspect I am a bloody shocking one – and that opinion is confirmed by the fact that I have never been asked to be godmother to anyone. Not one child.

Some of my girlfriends have 15 or so godchildren – seriously! – and actively hope that no one else asks them because they are running out of calendar reminders and the desire to send any more birthday cards and presents.

But not a single soul has trusted me with the care or upbringing of their child should they bite the dust. And, in some regards, I know where they are coming from. I have never turned up to an event with a Tupperware container, never made a fruit skewer from fresh watermelon and mango, and certainly never attended a parent-teacher conference out of choice. (I was coerced to attend on a number of occasions by my autistic daughter, a great believer in timetables and rules, who filled her timetable with meetings that she was then obliged to attend.)

Despite this, I still think I am perfectly at liberty to judge other mums because many of them are very bloody annoying indeed. Here's my top three.

1. Posh Mums, National Childbirth Trust, Upper East Side Mums

These are the sorts of women who do the weekly shop at Whole Foods – or at least send the nanny there to do it for them. Ever since they became double-income and comfortably well off as a family, and hubby was promoted in his hedge-fund business, the posh mum decides that she can't possibly give birth alongside other mums of poor breeding and low income, and joins private prenatal care. In the UK, it is called the National Childbirth Trust (NCT).

The NCT is essentially the childbirth equivalent of Nieman Marcus or Selfridges – a privately funded affair that ensures your vagina and its issues will never be within touching distance of any couples whose net income is less than $250,000 a year.

NCT mums get together at their private prenatal classes dressed in high-end maternity wear, and are immediately bonded for life, like breeding mares that know they are destined to be together forever. And many of them are – they are inseparable and move as one throughout the next 5 to 10 years of their lives.

Essentially, the NCT hits them at a very hormonal time of their lives when they are both fearful for the future of their precious new offspring (who, of course, are more gifted than any other children on the planet despite not being born yet) and shit-scared about how much this whole birth lark is going to hurt while wanting to show it because they come from horsey/farming stock.

Once they have finally popped out their little Anabella/Anastasia/Matilda/Jemima (insert name of private-school kid), they still mass together because they are now the bestest of friends, meeting up regularly at coffee bars and other outdoorsy places to overtly breastfeed using their enormous nipples or exchange recipes for vegan avocado cake.

I know of many old friendships that have been sorely tested by the arrival of the 'new' NCT mum friends, and completely sympathize.

It's not that you are jealous of them, although it has to be said that being well off does look mighty comfortable. But it is hard to believe that a group of women have formed such a strong alliance over the certainty that their vaginas are more equal than others, and their love of soft-jersey wear in primary colors.

I guess that I see childbirth as a leveller. It's something fundamental we are all able to do if we are lucky. They see an opportunity to buy a better kind of childbirth. Which doesn't quite sit right with me.

2. McDonald's Mum Mafia

Please understand: I love a good Big Mac meal with fries and a diet Coke. I really love the little packets of salt that make your kidneys wince, and the way the fries are usually a bit undercooked and droopy like an old man's appendage. Undercooked fries actually rock.

I even used to work there. I like to think I was the best drive-thru girl in the business. But the hardcore Saturday McDonald's mums scare the sh*t out of me.

Armed with massive Primark (think Old Navy) bags and dressed in stretchwear being tested to its limits, these massive women with their puffy kids in strollers congregate from 11:30am in McDonald's.

Having done their first round of unnecessary shopping for stuff they don't need, they are in for lunch with their kids and strollers.

They are terrifying – and not because they are fat and do this every single week. Or because all of their kids have a different dad and yet the same haircut. They are terrifying because they are depressing – somehow, this is all their world (and their kids') will ever be, and that makes me feel sad. It's so small as to be tiny, and yet they are so big as to be huge.

3. Vegan Mums

Vegan mums are a pretty new invention, given that no one was vegan back in the day when the world was a pretty reliable place – even as late as 1992. Of course, little vegetarians grow into adult vegans, and now we have to endure vegan mums. Frankly, it is one of the wonders of the world that these puny little half-people ever managed to get pregnant in the first place. They are so emaciated from their diet of quinoa and chickpeas that you'd imagine their ovaries had given up on eggs a long time ago and self-ingested them in a desperate bid to access some more protein.

First, given that menstruation (I hate that word) is all about iron, where are these bean-munchers getting their iron from if the last time they ate protein was sucking off a hippie called Philo from Extinction Rebellion?

And second, in order for their husky ovaries to have received the sperm, these women must have had sex. Or, in vegan speak: received a meat offering in their female front bottom.

Are vegans allowed to envelop male sausage? I hate to sound like a purist, but isn't that more 'flexitarian'?

My working theory – looking at the angry faces of most vegan mums – is that they achieved pregnancy via a handy sperm donor, a turkey baster, and one leg perched on the bathtub. I'd like to point out to these vegan loons that turkey basters wouldn't exist if it weren't for decent meat-eating types like us feasting on the pterodactyls at Christmas time.

Either way, vegan mums are terrifying, and their offspring have my undying sympathy and support. If ever I see a vegan mum with a child, I stare at it fixedly over its bean-curd-and-tofu-crap burger and encourage it to signal to me if it is in trouble. Like a hostage with its captor. Blink twice, kid, if you fancy some bacon, or Morse code SOS on the tabletop using your falafel. Let me feed you some cow!

I am all about 'live and let live,' being big on letting everyone do whatever they please, but I really do have to draw the line at vegan mums. If you want to starve your body of the stuff it needs and fill yourself only with vegetables and chronic flatulence, be my guest, but why force it on kids? Kids need bacon and roast beef.

I met a vegan kid – now an adult – who told me his upbringing was akin to child abuse and he still has issues with food and health now. My heart broke for him.

If you are the kid of a vegan mum, have been affected by any of the above issues, and need support but don't know Morse code for SOS, then e-mail me at katie@katiehopkins.co.uk – if your fingers are truly strong enough. If your bones are too weak, then drink milk from a cow until you are able to type.

Being a terrible mum

In truth, I have no right to mock these other mums. I am the opposite of what a mum is supposed to be, have never been part of the mums' coffee morning mafia, and wasn't sure I wanted a baby even when I was pregnant.

On discovering my boobs were bigger than they should be and I couldn't remember the last time I had a period, I took a test and knew the answer in my gut before I even saw the little blue line confirming my worst fears.

And so I lay down on my apartment floor and cried. A lot.

Then I moved to my default coping strategy of imagining 'this won't last', then 'nature will know best', and finally 'this will never happen'. I even ran the New York Marathon to help nature on its way, as if proving I was some kind of mad monster so Mother Nature would realize she had made a tremendous mistake.

To be clear, I would never call my pregnancy a mistake. We are all on a path – sometimes we have to be taught we are not in control.

I thought I was in control of my whole world. There is not a cat in hell's chance I would have stopped my job, my world, and my life to have a child at 28. I was living in Manhattan's East Village, earning a whopping great salary, and living a flashy life of nice hotels and fun dinners, with no reason to stop. I had everything a 28-year-old could want – and a whole lot more.

But you know what? In the blink of an eye I'd have been 46, probably unmarried or alone, and certainly childless, having spent the last three years trying to hump anything that moved in a last-ditch attempt to have a baby and prove that I was not as selfish as I appeared.

Chapter 6: Single and childless, could so easily and would so easily have been me.

But India arrived to save me from myself. She was a gift, and one of the greatest little human beings I know. The next chapter is all hers. She is a better person than me, and wiser, too.

My middle child, Poppy, is so much like me that my own father laughs hard at the thought, saying she is my punishment for being me at 14, enjoying the idea that I will now suffer the late nights of worrying about her safe return as Poppy asserts herself on the world – and, I fear, on half the young farmers in the West Country.

And my little one, Max, is going to be a heartbreaker, thanks to his father. He has white-blond hair, no sign of the Hopkins nose or cheeks, his father's body, and my legs, which makes me feel confident that he will be a 6-foot 5-inch beauty. As his mother, I will be beating off his sweethearts with a stick, whichever gender they may turn out to be. Frankly, he could go either way – or both.

He can dance, too, when no one is watching, although despite a solid campaign on my part to encourage him to be a ballet dancer and take lessons, he has refused. In retaliation against my ballet-dancing ideas, my husband buys him football kits as a defense mechanism against his Number 1 son being anything but a blond-haired, blue-eyed Ronaldo when he grows up.

It is not that my husband is some kind of anti-gay weirdo – he shops in Olebar Brown, for goodness sake, and has a penchant for a flat-fronted chino in baby blue.

It is more that football makes sense to Lovely Mark, and it's a language that he wants his son to be as fluent in as he is. Football is exclusively theirs, and I am happy for them, even if I do think Max in tights and a cod piece would be epic. My husband is a big fan of David Bowie, so why the leotard/stretchy-pants thing is such a problem for his own son, I have no idea.

Sitting here now, unsure of when I will be returning home and realizing it may be as much as 12 weeks before I see my children again, I understand that I am not a typical mum.

I have often put myself first, pursuing the ambitions I have to tell people truth from the road. It is not usual for a mum to leave her children for long periods of time or go to places where there's a real risk of being bludgeoned in the head.

But despite being 20,000 miles away, I can still tell you what my kids had for lunch, what my eldest thought of her shift at work, and what my young son has in his little daypack for tomorrow. I need to order name tags for Little Max and his school uniform; I just won't be there to sew them on. His dad will, however, so I am ordering the rubbish iron-on ones instead. There is always a way.

As their mum, I have made terrible mistakes; most of these cock-ups are catalogued in minute detail by the mainstream media. I have been fired from jobs, humiliated on the national stage, and been the source of headlines that would make Meghan the Stallion blush.

But I have come to realize that the art of being a brilliant mum is not to see myself as a mum at all, but rather as a person my kids can rely on – to be absolutely me.

Whatever you are, that's what they need – all of your flaws, your imperfections, your bad bits and good bits. They really don't care what other people think or write or say; they just care that you are doing the best you can for them, 100 percent every day.

And I know for sure that what I want for my kids has nothing to do with what other people want, any other measures of success, or any other child. I don't even want the same things for each of my kids; I want them each to connect in their own way with whatever makes them happiest. Anything that measures a kid is fundamentally flawed because it involves a common starting point, suggesting they are all the same. It's like standing on a tennis court and thinking all the balls will be coming straight to your racquet: you have to be prepared to move your feet to welcome them all differently.

If you're on the tennis court of motherhood and think you will be hitting back all of the parenting balls that come your way effortlessly because you dressed in the right outfit, attended a few dodgy classes, or read a couple of advice books, you are off your rocker. The starting point for each and every baby is so wildly different that you need trainers on and to get your feet moving.

One will be left field; one may be straight down the middle; and one will inevitably get caught in the net and need some help getting out. And if you spend any time looking around at other people's kids and listening to how marvelous they all are, you may as well smash yourself in your own face with your racquet and shove a tennis ball down your throat for all the good it will do you. That's why Facebook and chat groups are so beastly. So many mums try to elevate themselves by getting you to look at how brilliant their little Anatole is, or how their Benjamin has shot up and they're so thrilled that he's been made head boy and captain of the rugger team. They are trying to elevate on your envy, and that is grotesque. Face the other way and let them own their issues. Turn off their noise. Focus on your kids and where they are coming from and keep trying to bat them back roughly in the right direction. If you cock up, you do get a second chance.

I am living proof of that.

You might think your child needs a perfect parent but, in truth, all they ever want or need is imperfect you.

CHAPTER 8

HELP,
I'M NOT NORMAL

'I'm just going to pop out and grab another pair of eyes to look at this. Nothing to worry about, won't be a moment.'

If there is one phrase you don't want to hear when you are lying on your back, 36 weeks pregnant, with a nurse gliding an ultrasound across your protruding belly, it is this. No one needs a second opinion when everything is A-OK.

You know something is up when you hear the chirpy, cheery voice professionals use when they have seen something they know does not look good but don't want to give you advance notice that your whole world is about to fall apart.

It's a bit like an air steward crouching down to your seat level to tell you something; you are either getting kicked out of your seat or there is no chicken option left. Either way, the crouch means it's bad.

Lying here on my hospital trolley, the 'other pair of eyes' was clearly a bit of a dab hand with the scanner, and she busied herself pressing the probe against my huge stomach with clinical efficiency, clicking and scrolling and clicking to measure the important bits of the baby I was supposed to be cooking.

Her face was a picture of neutrality. I imagined her brain

shouting, 'HOLY FUCK , IT'S AN ALIEN!' while her face said nothing at all. That's quite a skill set inside the British socialized healthcare system.

I watched her, trying to work out for myself what was not right, wondering if her face would ever give away any clues. I could see and hear my baby's heart beating; that was the main thing, right? A heartbeat? Everything was all right as long as we still had that. Right? Right?

Wrong.

My baby's kidneys were too big, way too big – or, as one of the midwives put it, monstrous. If you are training to be a midwife by chance, please, could I just mention that 'monstrous' is not a word that should be used on a maternity ward, not ever. In hindsight I do wish I had gone back to see that woman one day and punched her in the tits.

Another midwife proceeded to demonstrate, in hideous detail, that my baby's kidneys were five times the size they should have been, bigger than her body would be able to cope with – certainly bigger than would fit inside of her own body.

I ask you to just imagine this for a moment: a baby, inside of you, nearly ready to come out, but with kidneys too big to fit inside its own little body.

I came to this scan to check my baby was normal. In the UK all pregnant women are given a hideous, wipe-clean Red Book when they are entered into the system, in which the NHS records all metrics related to them and their baby.

It always bothered me that it was so industrial-looking; just why this bloody book had to be wipe-clean I don't even want to think about. And why it had to be red of all colors – presumably to hide the bits of blood you are about to propel across the room at any given moment from your swollen vagina?

This damned Red Book follows you throughout your pregnancy, recording all the measurements and checks you've had, including your growing baby's height, length, and vital organs.

As I was only just beginning to understand, the aim is for you and your baby to be within the normal parameters for everything. There are sweeping graphs showing the upper centile and lower centile for everything: length, width, heart diameter, head diameter – everything. And, in a perfect world, you want to be tracking in the middle of those lines at every step of the way: weight, head size, leg size, heart, and lungs.

(And when I say perfect world I mean perfect according to the socialized healthcare system. And believe me, if they are the ones defining perfect, we are really f*cked. They pay $4.80 for a single roll of bathroom toilet paper because they are a bureaucratic nightmare.)

As a pregnant mum, the ambition is to be Little Miss Average, something I had never managed to achieve in my whole life thus far. So why I imagined it would be any different now, as I sat there in the maternity unit in stretch pants pretending to be a regular expectant mum, is anyone's guess.

For extra impact, the midwife trotted off and found some sheets of graph paper, attached them to the page of my Red Book where kidney measurements are recorded, and proceeded to create a fold-out section to the graph to really ram home just how off-the-chart and abnormal my baby was going to be – if, indeed, I got that far.

She literally demonstrated just how far off the chart the monster growing inside me actually was.

I can't quite explain what this whole experience feels like, but if you have been there or anywhere like it, you will know. I imagine it is like the doctor coming back with the face that tells you that your cancer isn't getting cured, or the vet's face when your dog didn't make it. Or a sinkhole opening up under your feet and sucking the ground away from your soul. It is the gut punch of finding out your husband cheated on you or the certainty you are about to be raped. It is on that scale of horror.

It is not like other broken stuff. If a plumber turns up at your house and tells you your boiler is broken and exactly which bits are at fault, it is a royal pain in the ass – especially if it is wintertime in the UK – but you suck it up, find out how much it is going to cost to fix it, and find a way to get your heating and hot water back on.

Other broken things can be mended – even your own broken heart, given time and enough energy.

But when it's a midwife and your eight-month-old unborn baby that you are talking about, it is a very different conversation.

The second visitor to your door after SHOCK is GUILT. What did I do? What did I not do? Was it my epilepsy tablets? Was it running the marathon? Was it wine? Women are world-class at this – not only emotionally loading up on their problems with their whole hearts but inventing layers and layers of guilt to go alongside the problems they already have.

With kind eyes (and less kind graphs), a very senior midwife is calmly telling me that my baby is a bit broken, only they don't know why or how to fix it – or what the broken bits will mean.

With the benefit of hindsight and many years of unpacking and processing this horror in my past, I now realize that this ultrasound scan and that bloody Red Book was one of the many times that I have let the British socialized healthcare system give me a bloody nose. Not only did I just stand there and take it, I kept bringing my nose back for them to punch again, and again.

I am not saying I should have argued with the nurses, who were trying their best – although as emotionally intelligently as a house brick. I am asking, what was the point of learning all of the questions if no one had the answer?

Essentially, my baby was not right. Over the next few days and weeks, a steady stream of pediatric specialists would tell me they didn't know what was wrong or why it was wrong, but that my baby wasn't looking good. Her kidneys were abnormally large, and these monstrous kidneys would probably be an indicator of something much, much worse, like a brain abnormality. I was told that a test of the amniotic sac that my baby was swimming about in was the only sensible solution.

So I agreed to have an amniocentesis test – taking a genetic sample of my baby and testing it for genetic deformities or conditions like Down's Syndrome.

These days I imagine all of this can be achieved through a blood test or something equally sophisticated, but back in 2003 the test that I signed up for was the stuff that nightmares are made of. A little gaggle of midwives (what's the collective term for midwifes – a cauldron?) jabbed a massive silver tube into my belly and then pushed it in a bit further to take a fluid sample from the amniotic sac that my baby was swimming about in. It is the stuff of Dr Frankenstein.

I do wonder whether doctors invent shit like this just to see how far they can push patients and test themselves. Medicine always wants to be 'advancing.' I am not sure many of these advances are actually taking us forwards at all.

I was warned that this test might result in a miscarriage. At the very least, it was an utterly miserable affair, risking my pregnancy for a nasty test to find out just how much of a monster my baby was going to be. I wish someone had stopped to ask me what I would want to ask my younger self now, if I knew then what I know now.

What will you do with the result? What if the test shows genetic abnormalities in your baby? How much 'abnormal' can you take? How much disability can you handle? Because, if your answer to all of these questions is to proceed with your pregnancy, and whatever information you gain is not going to change that, why put yourself through it at all?

What is the point of a test if you are not going to act on the result?

The problem with so much of what medicine has to offer is that it can tell you what is wrong but not why. Or tell you there is definitely a problem but without telling you a solution. As the best consultants will acknowledge openly to you, much of medicine is still based on the 'best guess.' And the best guess on the results for my baby was that she had a genetic abnormality – her genes were not lining up as they should, and she was missing a bit. In medical terms (as we would discover later), my baby had a HNF1B gene deletion, and it had presented on the ultrasound scans as abnormally large kidneys. But there could be much worse in store.

I was in Down's Syndrome territory. The HNF1B gene is a useful little critter involved in the development of kidneys, liver, reproductive tract, and pancreas, among other things. The letter that followed this discovery, from the pediatrician overseeing my case, didn't make for comforting reading. At eight-months pregnant, I sat down on a kitchen chair and read a letter from the consultant at the hospital, Vaughn, telling me that my baby:

- might not survive birth
- might only live one hour, one day, one week, or more
- might have multiple disorders, including an absence of, or defective, reproductive organs
- might be born with her kidneys outside of her body.

The letter offered me a late-term abortion and made clear that proceeding with this pregnancy was not advised. A man was telling me to abort my baby.

If you've never been pregnant, I should probably fill you in on what it is like with one month to go. Your belly is stretched so tight you genuinely fear the thing might burst when you sneeze (except that you pee instead). Your massive, leaky boobs fill all of the space between the top of your massive belly and your chin (or chins, in my case). There are many times every day when you genuinely struggle to breathe and wonder if your lungs have been rolled up like a sleeping bag to make space for your massive baby.

And, as you shuffle about like John Wayne at 90, you are certain that someone at the grocery store will be able to see your baby's head bulging out between your legs as you walk. Sometimes you have a little feel about with your fingers just to check this is not actually the case.

You are prone to peeing without warning; have hemorrhoids bunched like grapes in your ass, making pooping hard; and often spend the night wanting to stab anyone still able to sleep face down, or indeed sleep at all.

On the plus side, you can feel your baby jumping about inside of you like a maniac; you can see its little hands and feet poking out of your belly from the inside – and even try to tickle it back if you are quick. You and your baby are pretty much hanging out together as a little pair, kept apart only by a layer of skin on your tummy stretched tight like a drum, or by a steely membrane up your foof (aka vagina) that you can't help but be in awe of.

And, of course, there's all the stuff you have organized for this baby about to join your world. The little cot, the stroller, the car seat, and all the gubbins that go with preparing for a baby are now sitting waiting, smelling of newness and excitement. Not to mention a couple of grandparents – my own mum and dad – about to receive their first grandchild, busily handwashing sweet little knitted baby coats that were my 'great great great grandma's'.

You are all these things at eight-months pregnant.

A letter calmly offering you a termination is a hand grenade to the heart.

It wasn't until this letter was in my hands and the words 'late-term termination' were in black and white that I actually stopped to think about what a termination at eight months means. When something is written down, it changes; it is no longer words floating in the air in a room. It is written, and it is real.

What the hell even happens at a late-term abortion? I had naively imagined some clinical procedure where I would be unconscious under anaesthetic. I had chosen to imagine all of the syringes and nasty stabbing sensations would happen in the darkness of my unconscious, and I would try not to think about it, and then go home and get on with my life. These are the lies that you tell yourself when you really can't bear facing up to reality. It is definitely avoidance.

Avoid the pain in order to keep moving. It's something that has been with me my whole life and also explains why I was addicted to morphine at age 42. As much as we might scoff and say it is cowardice, it is actually quite a military strength, the ability to continue to fight forward when half your leg has been blown off, and perseverance is more important than pain.

The truth of late-term termination is that you have to have your baby. It sounds stupid to say, but how else is it going to come out? And, in having it, the baby is killed as it is born. You have to say it out loud to believe it could be true. I can still taste coppery vomit when I think about it; back then, it flowed out of me, wrenching my guts at the horror I was being offered by the medical profession.

Standing there holding a baby bump and a letter explaining how wrong she was is scorched into my being; that letter may just as well have been a branding iron.

I didn't know then what I know now. Agreeing to tests on your unborn baby leads you to this point. In the years before these 'medical advances', mothers wouldn't have known anything was 'wrong' with their baby and would have been merrily cracking on with being pregnant without any of this car crash I was living through in slow time. In times gone by there was less worry because there was less intervention. Admittedly, when things went wrong they went very wrong, but I suspect this remains true to this day.

In truth, I hadn't even wanted to be pregnant. I had never thought about having children, and I openly admit that I worked like a man and had a fairly male attitude to this stuff. Work always mattered more.

And yet, here I was, being told that my baby would be anything but normal, if she made it at all, and suddenly prepared to do anything to save her – this baby I wondered about even having at all in her earliest weeks, even running the New York Marathon at 12-weeks pregnant to see if she would somehow fall out.

Maybe I deserved this punishment for ever doubting her? Now all I wanted as I stood in my kitchen clutching this letter was for someone to tell me that my little girl would be okay.

But no one could. And there was my open and honest acknowledgement of myself, that I am not a good enough mum to be the mother of a disabled child. I am not patient enough, selfless enough, kind enough – just not good enough. And yet I knew I would not terminate my baby. I would fight this pressure to end it. I would face it, whatever it was. And I would just do the next thing next. If she lived one hour, one day, or one week, I would face it. And if she died the moment after I gave birth, I would face that too. I didn't know how, just yet. But I knew this much.

And I knew I could not face the alternative. I could not

be the monster that labored over a dead thing of my ending. I think, though, that if someone had told me they could click their fingers and magic her away, without horror or pain, and reset the clock to a time before I was ever pregnant, I would have gladly taken their offer. I wanted to wake up and find out this had all been a nightmare.

I was too cowardly to choose to live through the hell of terminating my living baby, but I was just as certain that I was not good enough to be a mum to a disabled child. Thus, caught between two evils, I was somehow responsible for both of them.

Perhaps I was being punished. Perhaps all I could do was take my punishment like a man. And so I did. I went to the hospital, refused pain relief, and delivered my baby.

My daughter India was born on 13 June weighing six pounds, looking as much like a little doll as anything I have ever seen. My father, her grandfather, was instantly smitten and remains so to this day. She is still his favorite, and all of the family knows it.

Perfect on the outside, with some hidden genetic mysteries on the inside (which we are still learning about and dealing with today), she was the opposite of the monster I was told to expect – a twist of organs and flesh, with kidneys outside of her body and unable to make it through a single day. Sixteen years on, she is living proof that medicine is often guesswork, and tests are only useful if you know what actions you are going to take based on the results.

I would like to take Indy back to that consultant and ask him to reflect on what advances in medicine really mean – and whether he would write that same letter to another mother in my position.

With the benefit of these sixteen years, I would never have had the scans or the amniocentesis test. I would never have known about India's gene deletion until it presented itself in other ways, and perspective would have lent me a hand.

HNF1B gene deletion is not without its complications. As with any gene abnormality in a child, there are always things that are less than ideal or that send you into spasms of guilt about what you have done to your child. I believe that my own epilepsy medication caused my daughter to suffer this thing.

As well as impacting the kidneys, the reproductive organs can be affected too. I spent many dark hours throughout India's early life wondering if she had a womb, whether she would be able to have children, how we were going to find out, and how we would break the dreadful news to her when it was finally discovered. I may have done this to her, too.

I will always feel responsible for anything she has to endure because of this condition. But I will always try to fix it, and perhaps this matters more.

In true Indy fashion, though, it turns out that her womb and all associated bits are in good working order; at least, that's what I understand from the mountain of sanitary pads constantly on display in the girls' bathroom, and their frequent updates as to their progress through 'period life'. My catastrophic scenarios of a devastated India learning she would never have children, played out over and over in my head, were all for nothing too.

Perhaps the most significant outcome has been Indy's autism, diagnosed very early and sticking her well and truly on the spectrum. Hers is not a difficult or behavioral form of autism, however; it's more emotional. Indy does not process emotions the way others do.

She didn't speak a word until the age of three, used to flap her little hands if she was distressed, seemed more prone to silence than to speaking. Even as a baby crying was not natural to India, and pain was foreign to her – and this remains so today, even when she has clearly been hurt. Indy does not really feel pain, and that is just as complex as a child who screams at a splinter.

I was sent to see a psychologist at Children's Health Unit for a formal diagnosis of India's autism. It still makes us giggle when we read the report of baby India's funny take on the world:

Q: What would you do if you saw a house on fire?

India: I would tell someone because that would be naughty.

Q: Why do policemen wear uniforms?

I ndia: Because it helps them look smart and being smart is good.

Q: Why do people cuddle each other?

India: To keep warm.

My funny, curly-haired, well-behaved child had gotten this far, so we were doing well … weren't we?

The psychologist sat me down to explain the side effects of the severe autism with which India had been diagnosed:

- A complete absence of emotional intelligence meant she would be ostracized and socially excluded due to an inability to communicate, and grow up with a sense of isolation and not belonging.

- She would be okay at primary school, where kids bumped

along with basic communication about food, fun, and parties, but by her teenage years she would rapidly fall behind the more sophisticated unspoken communication of her peers.

- In her later teenage years she would struggle to create relationships and secure work, which typically led people with India's kind of autism to suffer high rates of depression and suicide.

I was told my child would probably end up committing suicide.

India was five.

I can still remember the layout of his room, the smell of the chairs, the steep white stairs leading up to it, and my difficulty getting back down those stairs to get away from this hideous place. I had taken another bloody nose from the socialized healthcare system. And, once again, I just sat there and took it.

Why do they do this to a mother?

I endured the same through my pregnancy: she might not live; she might only live for a bit; she might live but be disabled; she might be born a freak show. Kill her if you want.

And now this. Now that I had my pretty, funny, polite, little thing, now I was told to believe she would be hated by others, left out in the cold, made to feel alone, ostracized as a teen, depressed for her best years, and suicidal as a young adult. I was told to expect to find her swinging from a tree.

The medical profession is merciless. I still loathe that psychologist and his diatribe of hate; to me, he is a monster, hiding in a suit and badge with letters after his name. Courtesy of this monster I spent more hours fretting and worrying. Would she kill herself one day? Would she be one of those lonely kids you see in an awkward anorak with acne, sitting alone on the bus?

I am sure there has been some of it. India told me about some of the treatment she suffered at the hands of her peers, after another classmate had left the school over bullying. She told me the other girls in the class had locked her in a room, pinned her down on a chair and held her there, laughing as they straightened her 'freaky' curly hair. I am sure there was more. Much, much more.

But she got through it, somehow. And India has come out the other side at 16 with more confidence, sense of self, and individuality than any other child I know. I am not saying this because she is my daughter. I am not bragging. I am saying this because she is Indy Windy and has proven them all wrong. All of them:

- the scanning team and their anxious eyes
- the midwives and their blasted Red Books
- the pediatric specialist and his push for termination
- the psychologist wanting her placed on suicide watch.

She has risen above every single one of them, and if you are me and have had this happen to you, your heart will burst as mine does with the pride of it all. Ours are the triumphant underdogs who went on to bite all those naysayers in the ass.

Every time she has been given the worst prognosis possible, she has simply kept on walking – kept moving forward, leaving them all behind standing empty-handed with their stethoscopes and lies. All of those awful hospital letters filled with terrible things I didn't want to hear seem to be fluttering at her feet as she swooshes on by. She is the definition of 'unstoppable'.

For all of the things that make your life harder as a high-functioning child on the spectrum – like not being given the secret key to how emotions work, or why you would go up and put your arms around someone for something called a hug, or what a smile means or a frown – there are equal and opposite benefits that become a shield against the worst that life throws at a young girl.

Young girls are the nastiest of sorts. I brought up my two girls with the mantra 'girls are weird' so it would be the default setting when other girls started being little assholes to them at school. Of course, every girl goes through this, whether it's being left out of this, excluded from that, uninvited to this thing, or gossiped about by that group over there.

The beautiful thing about not fitting in is that all of this is less troubling to India. She applies the purest unemotional logic and makes a rational decision, where a fully functioning teen (is there such a thing?) would apply emotion and angst.

Take, for example, a failure to be invited to a party when most others are. A regular teen would be floored, unable to withstand the humiliation, the unkindness, the cruelty. I have been there myself. I can still feel the heat in my cheeks when I was told why I was not invited to Zoe George's disco party – in case I wore horrible clothes. But India doesn't work by conventional rules.

Indy will recognize that it is a bit impolite to leave someone out when she is the only one not invited; she will consider the fact that she probably wouldn't have enjoyed it anyway; and she will wonder what she can do instead that might be more fun or better for her.

Take trying to get a part-time job. A regular teen would not be seen dead asking for a job, lacks real-life self-confidence to go into a store and open her mouth (despite her bravado online), and 'would rather die' than humiliate herself in front of another teen.

Indy will march on in, ask if there are any jobs, or ask who she can speak to about jobs. If she doesn't get a satisfactory answer, she will follow up by phone or e-mail and pursue it until she does.

Embarrassment, shame and humiliation are not on her register. It is a complete gift. She will stand butt-naked on a beach with her bush out to put on her swimming-cozzie. And when my other kids cry out with embarrassment, Indy will remark, 'They have a choice not to look; they are just devastated by my beauty.'

Employed as a Christmas elf at the local garden center, not only did India love the job and prance about as instructed by the elf leader, but she also wore that damned elf costume into shops to pick up takeaways and into pubs for a meal. So what if she was dressed as an elf? She was hungry and she had clothes on – so what was the problem?

Or stress, for example. Take a piano or violin exam. As a child I dreaded them with that sickening horror that made my mouth dry, my hands shake, and my most pressing decision – whether to shit or vomit – dire. Delightfully, such things don't even enter into India's thought process.

'Are you nervous?' I asked Windy as she waited for a difficult violin exam. 'Why would I be nervous? I am just here to show them what I can do,' she replied. Pure logic, void of emotion or reckless over-reaction.

For Indy, being autistic is not a disability. It is a gift, a sword, a shield, a complete way of life. It is like an elevation, where all of the nonsense stays well beneath your feet because you are superhuman, and emotional weakness is just not on your register.

During some of the most crippling or hurtful moments of my recent times, I have turned to India in the manner of a mother, trying to explain why I am upset, and she has given me the smartest advice of any soul on the planet. After a particularly brutal weekend of being attacked by the British media following an event I attended, I turned to India to try to explain why I was so hurt. I felt she was owed an explanation for my weakness. She solved the problem in under a minute.

Q: Did you do what you said you would do?
    Me: Yes.
Q: Were you happy with the work you did?
    Me: Yes.
Q: Did you get paid the fee you agreed upon?
    Me: Yes.
India: Then you did everything you said you would do. Anything else is their problem.

    Genius!

I love this amazing little person. I thought I was being punished, but in fact I was being taught – that the world is not one size. And I was given a gift of an amazing child.

I will always hate those Red Books. They are evil, trying to document 'normal' and make those who don't comply with that standard feel like a failure. Or worse.

In fact, I reject anything that measures, standardizes, looks for the average, or tries to tell me or anyone else what is normal. Anything that tries to compare my baby to yours, or how you are doing as compared to me, or monitors how I am progressing against whatever the system thinks is okay, riles me beyond belief.

So much of maternity and childcare is made of this evil. I blame starchy midwives from the 1970s with their white peak hats and bossy puff sleeves, and every single woman since who has somehow tried to elevate herself by being a perfect mother and posting pictures of just how perfect she is. Pregnancy is not a competition; there is no such thing as normal; and anyone who tells you otherwise is a freak.

India has taught me that there shouldn't even be a definition of 'normal' because, if we were all a bit more like India and those who have ripped up the rules of convention, we would live far better and happier lives. She is more powerful at 16 than I will ever be at 60.

Our family believes that all of the best people are weird. And if you feel you don't fit in, you are probably winning harder than you know.

Lessons from the Wise World of Windy
- Doctors do not have all the answers and are often wrong. Most of them are hoping to God they might be able to

Google the right answer to your problem and are actually just like you or me but in fancy dress.

- If you don't know why you need to know something, do you really need to know it? Don't have a medical test just because you're offered it. What's the point of having the test if you don't know what you will do with the answer? Work out the second bit before you have the first.

- Being average is not a measure and the '50th centile on a graph' should not be your ambition for your baby. Metrics and markers make you think it is important you fit in. It isn't.

- Children don't come from a Red Book. Who gets to decide what is 'normal'? Why is anyone even trying to measure it? How much interference do you need to cook a baby? Monkeys, cows and dogs manage it just fine. And their offspring are cute as hell.

- All the best people are weird.

- Never worry about the people who stand out; it's the ones who are desperate to fit in who have no spine of their own.

- Dress as an elf and go sit in a pub for a meal. India does it and it rocks. Strip naked on a beach to put your swimmers on. Make other people own their decision to look at you.

- Do not regard being uninvited as a snub. Consider it a free pass to do something a lot more fun.

- We are all on the spectrum; some of us just know how to work it better than others. If you aren't on the spectrum, where the heck are you? Get up here with the rest of us.

- Don't let doctors, consultants, or anyone you go to for advice give you a bloody nose. You went for help and information, maybe both. You didn't turn up so they could punch you in the gut a few times and break your face.

CHAPTER 9

HELP, I WANT TO STAB MY HUSBAND

We've all been there. Being married really isn't an easy thing. We spend half of our lives imagining we want to be married and half of our married lives wondering if we could stab our husband in the heart and get away with it.

Getting married and its sadder sister, getting divorced, is all stuff we willingly put ourselves through in the quest for happiness and contentment.

Lockdown has brought its own challenges, not least to marriages like mine where a good part of the reason the relationship worked was because both of us had separate lives outside of the house and interesting things to catch up on when we were back together.

I can distinctly remember sitting in my kitchen working and my husband, Lovely Mark, coming in to tidy the cutlery drawer. I visualized getting hold of the bread knife (he was also tidying) and ending him on the spot.

You could argue that tidying the cutlery drawer is a sweet thing to do, and perhaps you wish your husband would tidy things. But this was passive-aggressive tidying, indicating that I (a) am a lazy bastard who doesn't put things away properly, and (b) will now be forced to listen as my lazy-bastard ways are corrected.

It is in moments just like this that you find yourself wondering how it is that the start of your relationship – all hot dates, matching underwear and doing the nasty – has become a kind of duel to the death involving arguments about the vacuuming and the noise of the cutlery drawer being tidied.

I do not have the answer to a happy marriage, although I am pretty proud of the fact my second marriage has been far more successful than my first, and Lovely Mark is still speaking to me after 15 years or so.

When people find out I am married to Lovely Mark, they put on their best confused face and ask, 'You are married to Lovely Mark?' as if it is a physical impossibility that I am married to this quiet-spoken bearded chap who everyone thinks is Lovely.

Somehow – because I am supposed to be the Biggest Bitch in Britain and I sound a bit posh when I talk – strangers assume I am married to an asshole (like a wanker banker or a city trader). Finding out that my other half is a design dude and has an earring (and a skull for a wedding ring) is too much for my haters to handle. But it makes perfect sense if you start to get to know the real me.

He is also the guy in that field photo, which explains a lot. I think being caught having sex in a field with your fella is a good omen for any future marriage. We have been tested and through a lot together. Lovely Mark never left my side through four long months of brain surgery and recovery; he was right there when we thought it was the end and has helped me start I-don't-know-how-many new beginnings.

He is the first person I call when I am in trouble, and when I am not, and is the voice that has pulled me through dark nights on the road when things were not looking good for my sanity or my safety. And he somehow does all of it without being bitter or resentful.

My life, work, and decisions have always been unpredictable. But for as long as I can remember, Mark has told me, 'Work on the basis that it is a "yes", and we will figure out a way.' And we have – whether that was me disappearing off for Fidel Castro's funeral or spending three months on the road campaigning for President Trump.

I don't know how I got so lucky. But I do know I couldn't do any of it without him and often say as much on stage when I speak. People are kind enough to tell me I am brave, or I am fearless. But I know that I would not be close to any of those things if I didn't have Lovely Mark to take care of all the stuff that matters in my life, and to tell me it will be okay – even when it really isn't very okay at all.

Most recently, facing deportation from Australia for mocking their quarantine rules and being deliberately stress-tested by the government stooges in Immigration, in between periods of harassment, I lay in bed in the dark with a hot water bottle and my phone, messaging Lovely Mark. He was there for me at the end of the phone on the other side of the world, keeping me going, watching out for me every time the door knocked or the phone rang, helping to get me home.

I wonder why he does it sometimes; I wonder why he has stayed so long. I imagine how much easier his life would be with his first wife, no children, tennis holidays, spare cash to spend, and time to himself.

But I think we are just supposed to be together. We are opposites. He is quiet; I am loud. He is thoughtful and considered; I am combustible. He is detailed; I am slap-dash. He is rational; I am not.

We are an odd little pair. I love to dance; Mark would rather die. I think everything is a great idea; Mark knows better, but I can get the work of ten men done in a morning and have the family fed, watered, and out for a walk by 1pm.

It's not always easy being opposite. There is a chunk missing from our bedroom door where I slammed it so damned hard the latch ate into the frame. We have had romantic nights away that have turned into horror trips from hell and ended with us walking back to the hotel separately. I think I must be exhausting to be around. When I want something done, I want it done right away and I am not reasonable about it. My children acknowledge I need to go back on the road to give everyone a break.

But whenever I am home, Lovely Mark and I make plans to have lunch together and sneak out for pub lunches on our own. It is our way of making sure we get to spend some proper time talking about things we want to talk through, without the distractions of home, children, dogs, and work. It is our special time and my absolutely favorite thing.

When we have big things we need to sort, I make a list, and we go down to the pub with pen and paper in hand so we can rattle through stuff, both have our say, and decide what we are going to do – on anything from renovations to children, schools, or motorbike. Being apart as much as we are means we have to clear through as much as we can when we are together.

If I could distill our marriage into a single moment, it would be sneaking down the road to the local village pub garden, drinking beer and eating chips in the sunshine. Somehow, these moments make all the other moments okay. The children are increasingly keen to muscle in.

I wonder how it could be possible to have two such different marriages in one life – my first lasting less than a year, leaving me a little bit broken and a single mother of two kids under two years old, and the second one somehow mending everything. I wonder, could I have had the second without the first?

During one of our sneaky lunches, we were admiring the light fitting they had dangling over the massive stairwell, like a modern chandelier but with fancy lightbulbs and cables. I am drawn to light like a little moth and flit around the house at night making sure our lamps are on and candles are lit.

When I am alone on the road, before I go out, I turn on the lamps and TV so I don't come home to darkness. It's an Icarus thing, I guess.

In my absence on this latest road trip of mine, Lovely Mark is recreating the pub light we loved in our own hallway – building the fittings, wiring up the cables, and dangling brilliant bulbs about the place. He sent me a picture of his work in progress, and it made my little heart sing.

When people ask me how I do what I do or how I keep going, I think this is the best way to explain it: I can do this because Mark is doing that. When I am being hunted, or deported, or screeched at or hated, Mark is somewhere in my life stringing lights to our ceiling and making the world that little bit brighter. And when I turn to Mark and ask him what the hell I am doing all this for, he reminds me that I am doing just the same: stringing up lights, trying to make the world just that little bit brighter.

Learnings: Marriage 1

- Marrying yourself or someone similar to you seems to make sense in lots of ways. Actually, it's the equivalent of putting two male lions in the same enclosure. One is going to get killed.
- If you marry your boss, really try not to stay working in the same business. Having all your eggs in one basket – reproductively and financially – is not healthy.
- If you steal someone's husband, it does not necessarily follow that he will cheat on you – but you can hardly feel sorry for yourself when he does. Try and see it as a relay, with your husband as the baton. You have to pass him along.
- Do not marry someone old enough to be your dad. My husband was old and bald when we married; I was 28. Do all the nasty you need to do, but don't get married.
- Do not get married if you know it's not the thing you want most in the world, even on the day itself; that is still a perfectly good time to make a strong decision.
- Do not get married because you have a baby and think it is the right thing to do.
- Do not get married because someone asked in a big fancy way, and you don't want to disappoint them. A lousy husband is much more disappointing, I can promise you.

Learnings: Marriage 2

- Marrying someone opposite to you is smart. But there are times when you will want to stab each other in the heart for being so slow/fast, noisy/quiet, thoughtful/thoughtless.
- Always ask the other person to say sorry and tell them what you are asking them to say sorry for. And be sorry yourself, in return. This is a winning way to patch up issues of being opposite – and can be pretty funny. Lovely Mark will ask, 'What am I being sorry for?' and I can answer, 'So that I can be sorry too.'
- Tell each other that you love one other as often as you can.
- Hug each other as often as you can, even if you have to stop traffic or embarrass your kids to do so.
- Just because it's a good time for you and you really need to talk (on the other side of the planet) does not make it a good time for Lovely Mark, who is trying to handle home, kids, work, and cooking tea.
- If your husband is Lovely Mark and needs to be cross, but does not explode like you do, you have to work out how to pull his pin out. No one wants to walk around with a primed grenade.
- Occasionally, send rude pictures to your husband at inappropriate moments in his life.
- Definitely have children. Nothing has made Lovely Mark happier on this earth than his son. It's the best present that I ever gave him.
- Make talking a thing; date night is overrated, but talk lunches in the sunshine help keep you on your path together and to get sh*t done.

- Try to have separate bathrooms. Lovely Mark and I share ours, but it's good to have relationship goals.

CHAPTER 10

HELP, I DON'T KNOW WHAT TO DO WITH MY LIFE

As I write, many of our beautiful healthcare workers are being fired for refusing to take the state injectable, otherwise known as a vaccine. In New York teachers have been told they must take it or they too will lose their jobs. This is a whole other level of awful.

You cannot rationalize with the irrational, and firing amazing care workers whom our elderly depend on is an act of gross negligence. I pray that those holding the line and refusing to have the injection for their own reasons will be rewarded in the end.

I understand what it feels like to be fired – although for less noble reasons; I am not a good enough person to be a care worker.

But I have been fired more times than most, and undoubtedly more times than you. In fact, I have been fired so many times that Chapter 10 became two chapters. Which is deeply shaming in itself.

Being fired a lot is not something I am proud of, and it is certainly not a claim to fame. But it is a fact of my working life and, given that most of us fear being fired more than we fear death, I do have the experience to offer some well-tested advice.

Most of this advice is based on our agreement that you are

not trying to be like me, nor should you be. My life is not a format for long-term job stability or job security.

For that, you want my sister-in-law, who has worked at the same job all her life, in the same building, and can easily retire early if she wishes. She has a big fat pension she can depend on, has accumulated paid holidays and sickness leave for the last 30 years, and now has more paid holiday leave per annum than days she is required to work.

There is a great deal to be said for this approach to life. I doubt she has spent a single sleepless night wondering how on earth she will find employment again. I strongly suspect she has never felt guilty about taking a holiday because, when you are on payroll, it's a perk. And I don't think for one minute she has ever had to ring her boss and inform him that tomorrow she will be seen (in the national papers) naked in a field straddling another woman's husband, and that perhaps Human Resources ought to be informed.

I have made this call. And it was mighty sweaty.

There is a lot to be said for traditional employment. I am reminded that the first proper contract I ever signed committed me to 35 years in the British Army Intelligence Corps. These 'regular commissions' were incredibly rare, and it was and remains a real honor to have been considered worthy of one. I promised to dedicate my whole working life to the service of my country, and I meant it. And I still do, in fact. As I see it, my service to my country is ongoing – just not with the same employer.

If things had turned out how I had hoped and promised, right now I would be striding about manfully somewhere, rocking a beret and boots and saving the free world. But that was not to be, as we will discover later.

I promised the men who hired me that I would be the first female general and would stay loyal to my men until I was 60. This is what I call the straight-line approach to life: you set your sights on something and work towards it – systematically and rigidly, without deviation – until you get to the end.

My father did exactly this, working his whole life for one company, even as his job got further and further away from our family home, until he retired. He used to sleep overnights in a cheap B&B in a different city to break the number of hours he spent travelling in order to keep that job. And he slept on the floor of the control room during the night shift so he could come back home early the next day. It was a safe and reliable job, and he kept it by doing what he was supposed to do and accepting all the stuff that comes with keeping bosses happy. That required a self-discipline and control I do not have, and I admire him hugely for it.

Despite being brought up in a council house with nothing to call his own, my father put me and my sister through private school and university with the 24/7 assistance of my mother, who cared for all of us full-time so we would all do better together. He sacrificed a lot for all of us.

But despite trying to emulate my father and signing up for a 35-year straight-line career, the opposite has turned out to be true in my life. I am about to take you on a whistle-stop tour of the most awful moments of my career. Your life will seem perfect by comparison.

You may have used the expression 'I wanted the ground to

open up and swallow me'. At times, I have wanted a handgun with a single bullet.

I should start by saying this was not always the case. I have had jobs that did not involve me being fired and marched out of the door accompanied by security, the press, or both.

Buns and burgers

If you will allow me to brag for a moment, I was an extremely successful Wimpy waitress. Aged 14 and clad in bright-red dungarees that acted like a cheese wire on my private parts, I worked at the Wimpy burger bar on Saturdays, pocketing a terrific £1.40 ($2) per hour serving their famous Bender in a Bun to unsuspecting diners, with my camel-toe cleft asunder at their tabletop.

I gracefully resigned from this highly rewarding position when I secured a stint at the local bun shop, which I proudly held onto for a good few years. The owner had me pay myself directly from the till and pay the rest of the young people I was somehow watching over. As the unofficial Saturday Bun-Shop Queen I spent many a happy shift gadding about with the other young staff, gossiping with mates who popped in to say hello, and making eyes at the delivery lad, Chris, who, for the longest time imaginable, remained oblivious to my charms. Obviously he buckled in the end. They all do eventually.

I was not fired from this job either, but buggered off to Australia for a year to become an exchange student at Pennant Hills High School and wear the actual Home and Away uniform. That's a whole other book right there.

At college I was the McDonald's drive-through girl and

am very proud to say I was awarded a Gold Star for my sheer brilliance at pleasuring drivers as they passed through my window. On one shift the area manager came around and was very excited I knew the reason why we folded the brown bags to seal them before handing them to the customers. I told him it was to keep the heat in, and he looked at me like I had just discovered the theory of relativity.

This is the genius of McDonald's: it has created a system so devoid of the need to think for yourself that the thickest and the most gifted are absolutely equal, much like basic training in the army. If you take away the need for a person to think and drill rules into them instead, life goes a lot more smoothly. When something goes wrong you don't have to think of what to do because it's a reflex drilled into you over and over. I mean this kindly: if you are thick as mince, work at the military or McDonald's. Both are brilliant.

Arguably, the ages of 14 to 17 years were in fact the most successful of my career. I held multiple positions in a number of different industries (mostly related to burgers) and left with nothing but kind words from my bosses or an extra handful of cash. I didn't even catch a venereal disease from another staff member, which is surprising in itself.

There is an argument that I am best suited to dead-end or low-wage jobs with little or no responsibility, as I fared rather well in all of them. The truth is, I needed to earn my Saturday cash to be able to go out and have fun at the weekend. Equally, it is probably quite hard to get fired from a job that pays £1.49 per hour, where your bosses are delighted if you are good enough to show up.

I was not yet known. Being well-known changes everything.

The British Army

Technically I was not fired from the British Army; I was medically discharged. And as a salve to this wounding, I completed officer training at The Royal Military Academy Sandhurst and received the Adjutant's Medal for Athletic Achievement before I was booted into touch. I can hold my head high knowing I was good enough. And I remain the only epileptic ever to have made it through any Military Academy.

At the risk of blowing my own horn, I was a bloody useful Army officer. I could run faster than most of the boys, was the Army's 800-meter runner, was selected to compete against American cadets at West Point (their Sandhurst), and was engaged all the while to another Officer Cadet, Neil, whom I love very much to this day.

But whichever way you parcel it up, and however much I try to hide it with my Hopkins humor shield, being discharged from the military was and remains the most painful moment of my life, and I have carried that pain with me all my subsequent life as well.

I suspect that this helps explain a great deal of my behavior (good and bad) and actions since. And when people ask me if I have any regrets in my life, I know it is this. But I laugh and tell them no because if I were to confess the hurt of all of this, I would be reduced to a tiny thing in an instant. I keep it shut away in a safe, triple-locked, without knowing the code.

It's too hard for me to write here. Being fitted for my Intelligence Corps mess dress but never getting to wear it in my own mess; having my grandfather come to my passing-out parade but then never making it to my regiment; the fact that it became a non-topic when I returned home, and no one spoke of it or of how I felt – I was just the embarrassing daughter who came home when she shouldn't have, which didn't sit well with the 'good news' my mother liked to tell the family.

I daren't so much as scratch the surface of all this, as I fear what might come out. I have been keeping it all in for decades. It's a wound I cannot heal.

This was the job I should have had for life, and this was the life I had wanted. And the only thing that separated me from it was my epilepsy. Having seizures is not compatible with being an officer in the British Army. In my infinite wisdom I have come to recognize that being an epileptic with a semi-automatic weapon was not my finest idea. I joke about this in my speeches when I explain away my past, as if I am not hurt by it – funny Katie, performing like crazy to avoid the pain of the thing.

But I know that was where I was supposed to be. When I am near ex-servicemen and -women, no one needs to say anything; we immediately fall into step. We have the same groove; we speak the same language, physical and comedic. The military is in my bones and my sinews; I don't know who put it there, but it will never leave me. And I will always miss what I never had, even to this day. Maybe it's what I have always been trying to replace, and perhaps it's what drives me to 'man up' and face down those whom I see as the enemy.

It is curious that, despite (a) being the least humiliating of my departures and the most 'respectable' in the sense that having epilepsy is a condition, not a choice, and (b) arguably, being medically discharged is not the same as being fired, this was by far the most painful.

I hold onto the knowledge that I made it through the Academy because it is the only way to stop it hurting more than it does. Maybe unpacking it like this on paper is part of the healing that we all need to do. HELP may be helping me to survive a bit better at life too, and I have you, the reader, to thank for that.

Management consulting

Working at a management-consulting firm is a pretty glamorous life in many ways. There are business-class flights, and a lot of staying in nice hotels and turning up in boardrooms in suits and heels.

It is even more glamorous if I think back to younger me in my labia-splitting red dungarees at the Wimpy Burger Bar being paid two bucks per hour at age 14. Ten years later I was unstoppable.

McKinney Rogers is a management consultancy that, bluntly, helps people get sh*t done. If the boss decides the company is going to do such-and-such by this date, McKinney Rogers is brought in to help make it so and to get Brian in sales & marketing to understand exactly what his part in the plan is going to be and why he is going to make it happen.

McKinney Rogers was also exclusively filled with former military men, most of whom had been Marines of fairly high rank. Being the only female consultant on a team like this had a cachet all of its own – overseas travel, a team with the operational efficiency of a Tesla, and the attention that comes with being the only Sheila – or Doris, as my husband would say.

I fit in with my military peers like a plug in a socket and, as a result, my career inside the firm progressed at double-quick time. I whizzed up the rungs of the ladder like so:

- posh secretary with more formal educational qualifications than most of my bosses
- junior consultant who turned out to be really good at presentations and reading a room
- senior consultant who could be substituted for the boss, be entertaining as well, and deliver a two-day workshop at the board-of-directors level in a few languages
- sex slave to the married boss (despite the certain knowledge that many others had been down that well-trodden path before)
- wife of said boss, VP of Marketing, with a luxury pad in the East Village on 14th Avenue, and working on Madison Avenue and 52nd St.

I had arrived!

When I reflect back on my time at the company, I have so many happy memories – especially in the early days when I was gadding about like a wild thing, running conferences for global brands with a team of strong lads by my side, motivating and engaging audiences of corporate boards. And in the latter days, when I was setting up an apartment in the East Village with my partner and future husband (and CEO of the business), both of us were having the time of our lives.

I think it is really important to bookmark the amazing stuff that happens in life. What happens to it later should not change how you feel about the great bits you loved.

But things change, and people move on. This is a rather kind way of saying that my husband had another affair, with the secretary, and left me with two children under the age of two.

Please HOLD your outrage.

You may be somewhat inclined to be outraged on my behalf at this point. Who the hell leaves their wife with two children under two? And for the secretary? Puhleeze.

But before we get too carried away on Team Katie, let's remember that my husband was married when I met him. When we upped sticks from the UK and were living the high life in Manhattan, his first children genuinely thought he was dead; he simply disappeared from their lives, overnight.

So there are many bad guys in all of this, and I was one of them. I am proof that what goes around comes around.

But I think it is also fair to say that trying to be a Senior Consultant at a firm where your boss is your husband and father of your two children, and is furiously rogering the secretary, and everyone in the firm knows about it but doesn't have the heart to tell you, is not a tenable position.

My position as extremely humiliated wife-employee was untenable.

I stuck it out for a bit, mostly out of sheer steely will. I guess he hoped I would shuffle off quietly into my house, feel sorry for myself and never show my face again. And, believe me, I wanted to.

So I did the opposite.

What could be more awkward for the staff than to have me in the office working for their boss (also my husband) who was now living with the secretary in my apartment in New York City – it is as gruesome as it sounds. The secretary even packed up my stuff and sent it back to me, as if she were just taking over an apartment from a dead woman.

Perhaps one of my saving graces was that I somehow managed to channel this hurt into the gym; having two kids back-to-back gave me incentive enough. I was still being paid a significant sum for a job I didn't have to show up for – on account of it being terrifically awkward for all concerned and my husband being a git – and I needed to do something to save my sanity.

My six-pack abdomen said more about my marriage and my attitude than words ever could, and I am so happy it was the gym – not gin or wine or cocaine – that took the brunt of my anger. I am not certain the same would be true now at nearly 50 years old.

The kindest among us will acknowledge that I was not necessarily fired in the traditional sense but rather was unceremoniously and brutally made 'surplus to requirements'. The French have a saying: when you marry your lover, you create a vacancy.

Damn the French for being right all the time! And better looking. And gloriously slim. The body I built off the back of my husband's vulgarity is the same one I rely on today when things get tough. Training is an investment.

When I was finally ready, I handed in my notice, cleared my desk, and left.

I was sad for the job that I used to love and many of the friends I had made there. I still have to guard against looking back in idle moments and thinking about all of them knowing my husband was sleeping with someone else when I was eight-months pregnant. But I was relieved to finally step away and begin to start again, again. Little did I know that worse was yet to come.

Learnings
- Have as many shitty part-time jobs as you can and as much fun as you possibly can in doing them. These are the times of your life that you will remember. Some of my best memories come from the crazy jobs I did as a kid.
- Definitely hang out with riff-raff if your mother tells you not to do so. People who are 'beneath you' can often teach you the most.
- Always try to work with military men, at least once in your life.
- Do not let your condition define what you can and cannot do, even if you know it is 'not allowed'. The things we love the most may hurt the most, but that does not make them wrong. Sometimes you have to go balls to the wall to build yourself stronger.
- Epileptics who make it through the Royal Military Academy Sandhurst rock!
- Really try not to marry your boss.
- You spend a lot of your life working, so unless you are my sister, you may as well spend that time doing something that makes your heart sing.
- Don't look back and try to look forward at the same time – your head will wobble and fall off. When you are ready, always move forward, never back.

CHAPTER 11

HELP, I'M BEING FIRED

Are you noticing something of a theme here? Can you believe that I am only 46 years old? People say I look older and I say, 'Is it any bloody wonder, with the life I have lived?'

I have been fired a lot, and some of those experiences have been seared into my soul. But I have actually been fired a lot without actually being fired: the Royal Military Academy Sandhurst (medical discharge), McKinney Rogers (husband went off with the secretary), and then The Apprentice. I wasn't actually fired there, either; I told Lord Sugar to stick his job and walked off the set. But the outcome was pretty much the same.

I know I am accountable for all of this. It is very fashionable, particularly among the young or abrasively female, to imagine that I had no role in any of these things, that I was simply a victim of misfortune and that everything is unfair. Life can be unfair, cruel even; I would argue that being born with epilepsy is damned unfair. But I don't think that attitude is helpful and, usually, somewhere along the line, I made a decision or a choice that most would consider wrong, which led to the next thing.

So you could try to be a Katie ally and argue that being kicked out of the British Army was 'not her fault', and you'd have a point. I certainly proved myself physically capable because, clearly, I am still not over that whole failure. I knew there was a possibility that I was epileptic when I applied – I was even having seizures while I was there. The decision to hide my epilepsy and pretend to be okay does sit with me; I am accountable. I would not change my decisions even now, but I am still accountable for the outcomes.

Right, back to the gory details:

The Apprentice

I used to work at the UK Meteorological Office, the government and military body that predicts the weather in the UK. I know, it seems unlikely – partly because I'm not a scientist, but mostly because I have some semblance of a personality and this sounds like the dullest job on the planet.

I was recruited to run the consultancy business in the commercial arm of their organization, responsible for actually making money and bringing some profit back into the company – a groundbreaking idea for many of those happily being paid by the state.

It was a big job and well paid, particularly so for a job in the southwest of England where most jobs don't break the £20,000 per annum ceiling. Selection is my thing; my CV reads like a scorching rocket thanks to years in the international consulting scene in New York City and London. And I had the personality to pull it off; later this personality would prove to be my undoing.

Just to reflect on my status in life at this point, I had been dumped by my husband and unceremoniously kicked out of my job by his mistress, had two daughters under the age of two years old as a now-single mum, and was severely epileptic. I kept all this information to myself.

You would think that scoring a high-powered, well-paying job just miles from my country home with all the challenges in my personal life would be a moment to celebrate, settle down, and get my life well and truly in order. Maybe I could spend time with my babies? Maybe I could try and rest up in between my work and seizures? Any rational woman would have hunkered down and made the best of it.

But no, while applying for this big power job as Head of Business Consulting at the Met Office, I also completed an application form to be on the British version of Donald Trump's The Apprentice. For clarity, the British version of this show is nothing like the American one. There is no Donald Trump, just a shirt man called Lord Sugar. I don't believe there is actually a real job on offer, and the other candidates appeared to have been selected from some breeding farm for smooth brains.

In typical Hopkins fashion, I was selected from 25,000 applicants, so I asked my new boss for a leave of absence from my new job as Head of Consulting at the prestigious UK Met Office to go and try my hand at reality TV.

Off I went, a single mother of two children under two, having given up a high-paying job near my own home in the West Country in exchange for the uncertainty of filming a TV show in London for eight weeks unpaid; with no access to phones, cash, or freedom; living in a house with twelve strangers; and watched over day and night by a minder. The minder even stood outside the door of the cubicle in the bathroom. The sense of being someone else's property was very real.

It does make me wonder what on earth I was thinking. What was I on? Some kind of mission to prove I was invincible? To whom, and for what? What else could I have done to show I was tougher than the rest, stick a broom up my ass and sweep the floor as I went?

I was a fully epileptic mother of two, with a mortgage and no partner to rely on. What the hell was I doing?

You know, I bloody love that 30-year-old me. If she could see me now, I'd scream, 'Yaaaas, you go girl, you show 'em', the way I do when I see another runner on the beach (true story). I'd say, 'Damn girl, you got balls.'

I am drawn to the sheer energy of this decision. Imagine it: no husband, no one to tell me it would all be okay, two little people needing everything done for them, a big job with demanding bosses and a team of 50-odd persons, and still somehow deciding to go off to film on a show I had never watched, in an industry I didn't know, on a program whose entire raison d'etre is to make people look like fools.

It is easy for me to reflect and think what an utterly mad and selfish thing it was to do. It is pretty easy to be wise now about why all of this was a bad idea or to come up with a million reasons why I shouldn't have done something like this. But I don't smirk at the 30-year-old me and think I know better now; actually, quite the opposite. I am standing on my chair admiring her sheer bloody ballsiness.

I don't look back with regrets, and I certainly wouldn't change anything, even as I am about to share the levels of devastation and humiliation that I brought into my life.

If anything, I worry that now I would not be as bold.

Let's hit fast forward.

I thought I would be let go from The Apprentice somewhere near the middle of the show, looking like a pretty good egg, and trot back to my big job with a few fun stories to share with friends. I have never been more wrong.

I had more screen time than any other candidate, was offered my place in the final, and then created an unholy shitstorm when I turned the offer down, in front of 12 million viewers. There was no way I was going to sit quietly for six months working in a fabricated non-job while we all waited for this program to go to air. So I fired the boss.

Now, back at work as a serious Head of Business Consulting at the UK Met Office, my series of The Apprentice was airing on TV. My bosses, my team, and my customers had eight weeks of my face on prime-time BBC.

My bosses endured eight weeks of me saying things you simply cannot say, crucifying people straight to the camera, and being as badass as it is possible to be. The media circus around me was at Las Vegas levels; my private life was splashed across the front pages; and, to top it off, a particularly tenacious press photographer snapped pictures of me having sex in a field with my latest squeeze.

I don't do things by half.

My bosses needed to fire me, and they did it in the most bum-clenchingly awful way possible. Get your popcorn, because this is nasty.

Getting fired from my proper job

I did not have a good feeling when I rocked up for work that Monday.

The noise around me was at hysteria levels; I was being tailed by the press; there were front-page pics of me having sex in a field; and, rightly or wrongly, I was now officially The Biggest Bitch in Britain.

None of these are entirely in keeping with a prestigious scientific institution that prides itself on intellectual rigor, academic study, and studious silence.

I remember striding up to the huge glass door of the building, putting on my best brave face, and hoping the rest of me would catch up. I scanned my security pass and slammed straight into the turnstile – that turnstile was not going anywhere. I tried to act casually surprised and smiled cheerily at the receptionist, who told me to take a seat. She told me someone was on their way down to meet me. I should have upped sticks and walked out of the door right there and then.

If the receptionist had been a decent sort, she would have saved me the humiliation of walking into the turnstile. But I suspect she rather enjoyed her big moment and recounted it to her friends later at great length. It is an ugly truth that some people salivate at others' shame. If this had happened in the age of the mobile phone, one of the little bastards would have been filming it all, and it would have been up on the pages of the leftist rag The Mirror before I had even left reception.

My boss came down, asked me to follow him, and led me in silence to the power room on the top floor of the building, where an assembled throng of senior executives and lawyers was gathered. While considerably less dramatic, I now have some understanding of what it must feel like to be a Muslim woman in Iran about to be stoned to death.

All of these people were here to throw rocks at my head, and boy did they look as if they were enjoying it. My boss told me I was fired, with immediate effect. I don't recall the specifics of the crimes that had aggrieved them so, but I do remember hearing a few of them and knowing they were administratively inaccurate. But these were minutiae; the details were irrelevant.

What was I going to do? Fight my way back into an organization that didn't want me there? Make the case that, despite my nipples appearing in a pointed fashion on the front page of the news, I was still a credible face for their organization? Tell them that the Biggest Bitch thing would all die down in a couple of weeks?

They wanted me out; they had a point; and I would not give them the enjoyment of a reaction.

But it got worse – much worse.

Like some spine-tinglingly awful episode of a drama that you don't want to be cast in, security arrived to escort me to my desk on an open-plan megafloor with a hundred or so people, with all of my staff watching from behind their screens, pretending to be busy.

I remember feeling glad I had made an effort with my power outfit, even though a bead of sweat had just run down my inner thigh. Perhaps it was actually pee, but what woman would be expected to know the difference in these circumstances?

I was handed a black bin bag (aka trash sack). In my heels,

suit and best power hair, I had to throw the contents of my desk into this bin bag with my security detail watching my every move.

I could feel a thousand pairs of eyes on my soul. I don't honestly know what I threw in that black plastic bag but I know there was stuff in it because I had to carry it across the floor like some redundant Father Christmas with depression.

I was taken to the fire escape, shoved out of a side door, and told to leave the premises. I did the walk of shame to my car, put my sad little trash sack of stuff in the back seat, and drove back to my home. The Met Office had put me out with the trash, quite literally.

It was crushingly awful. 'Humiliation' is not a big enough word for what I endured.

But I did not show emotion, I did not speak, and I did not lose it. I did not cry. I adopted a dignified face and stuck with it for the whole horrendous half-hour, and when I walked out of that building and to my car, I walked like I was hitting the catwalk in Paris. I got all the way home before I exploded in a heap of tears, piss and vomit.

Public dignity, private death – sometimes that is all we have.

Learnings

- If your security pass at your place of employment suddenly stops working and the receptionist looks like she has a large aubergine shoved up her bottom, prepare to be fired and get your game-face set. Be ready to perform harder than Evita.
- Wear your hottest underwear, your sexiest shoes and your highest hair. Arm yourself with all that you are.

- Go full arrest mode. Yes, please. No, thank you. No answer. Cull all that is unnecessary. When everybody is watching to see your suffering, don't give it to them. Be vanilla. Load your bin bag like you are loading groceries and walk out like you are on your way to a dress fitting. You are the ice queen, and you will not give them your power. Wait until you are in your car to puke, shit yourself or cry. If you do all these three things at once, consider writing off your car and buying a new one.

Being fired from The Apprentice

After nine weeks of relentless filming, imprisoned in The Apprentice house, chaperoned at all times and denied phone calls to my small children or my family, I ended up making it right to the end of the show and was offered my place in the final.

The producers had discovered I was TV gold (I had no idea) and therefore kept me in the process. I was speaking my mind about the other contestants directly to the camera without a filter and with a particularly cutting turn of phrase, and had become the biggest character on the show.

The final five were on their way to the last 'boardroom' filming. We all drove out to the pretend boardroom (actually a mocked-up room in a massive hangar) and trundled in with our empty suitcases bouncing along behind us, to be patiently told by the pretend secretary in the pretend office with her pretend phone line attached by a cable to absolutely nothing that, 'Sir Alan will see you now.' (In America, this would have been Donald Trump.)

I still didn't know what I was going to do. My gut said I wasn't getting fired, and that I would be given a place in the final.

I had two babies at home that I hadn't seen for over two months. My family and nanny were feeling the strain of coping on their own. I had a well-paying job to get back to. I was not going to sit in a festering part of England (Brentwood) for four to six months waiting to film a finale, putting my whole life on hold waiting for a TV program to be aired.

And so I sat opposite Sir Alan and waited, hoping the decision would be taken out of my hands and I would be fired. But it wasn't; I wasn't; he picked me first for the final.

As I sat there sweating about just how bad a decision this was, why I really shouldn't be doing this, and why I needed to get back to my life, he came back to me; a producer will have alerted him to the fact I had a face like a slapped ass.

'You just got your place in the final but you look like I gave you a place at the funeral! What's going on?'

I thanked him and the team for the experience, explained that I felt the others in the room were more desperate than me, got up, excused myself, and left.

The executive producer was outraged; the series producer and production team were apoplectic. I got sent outside to think about my actions. We all had to take a break while thoughts were had.

I was asked to change my mind – I wouldn't. Someone more senior tried to persuade me to change my mind – I wouldn't. I was allowed to make one phone call home. My father said the family needed me back, so that was the decision I made. I agreed to reshoot the scene, to make Sir Alan look more in control and me less so.

I walked out of the British Apprentice, the first candidate to fire the boss. The sh*t was about to hit the fan … and it was set on high.

Learnings

- Sometimes, things have to come down to the wire for you to get your heart to speak up. Trust it! I was in the most awkward situation imaginable (being watched by 12 million viewers when this moment appeared on TV), but my heart still prompted me to do the right thing when it mattered. Trust in yours. The Apprentice put a hand grenade in my life, which changed its trajectory – completely. Life teaches us to take the safest option; perhaps sometimes we all need to resist that a bit more.
- I want to harness more of this spirit, bring it forward with me, and cast it out to others, whatever we might call it: being foolhardy, having cajones or chutzpah, foolishness? Probably a little of all these things.

But what a happy thing for the younger me to have had that courage! And how much better are all those things than what I fear we are cultivating in our young today: fear, anxiety, self-consciousness, a clinging to safety, and the endless encouragement to stay at home.

I am not trying to blow smoke up my own ass here, rather to use my younger self to remind us all why going balls-to-the-wall is an art we need to hold onto.

It is easier to do risky stuff when you are young because you are less spoiled. As we get older we get fatter, more set in our ways, and less flexible – in every sense. It is a great pity. I still love this 30-year-old me and, if you are in any way young, I hope you read about my splendid disasters and feel encouraged to produce many more of them yourself.

Being fired from my radio show

'Katie Hopkins has left the London Broadcasting Corporation by mutual consent, with immediate effect.' That was what the press release said, but it was absolutely not true. I didn't 'mutually consent' to anything. I was shot at point-blank range by my boss and his legal sidekick, and I had to drag my bleeding carcass out onto the streets of London to work out what had just happened in that small room where I used to work.

It had been a horrific weekend in London with yet another terror attack, and I was raging when I took to Twitter to declare, 'We need a final solution to terror.' I meant the words exactly as they are intended to be used – as in, never again.

But that one tweet was enough to get me fired from my beloved radio show and just about everything else. It was the Ultimate Cancel Card my adversaries had been looking to play since I became one of the most successful and well-paid journalists in the mainstream media.

Of course, I had meant a lasting solution, one that stops terror attacks on our kids once and for all. But in today's world of wokedom, you had better not be a white Christian woman using language perceived to reference the Holocaust – even on a subject that has NOTHING TO DO WITH the

Holocaust and is specifically about ending ISLAMIST terror attacks in the UK.

Regardless, I gave them an open goal and they booted the ball into the back of the net.

The British left-wing newspaper of the powerful (The Guardian) coordinated a campaign to have me canceled from everything. It was brutal and effective – and a good five years in advance of the 'cancel culture' that has become all-pervasive across the UK and USA.

They lobbied advertisers to pull advertising, had political and other contributors sign to say they would not appear on LBC (London Broadcasting Corporation) again unless I was fired – which was particularly effective because radio shows need guests. And, of course, many high-powered editors at competing networks were best mates with the owner of the station. For me, the noise was deafening.

At times like these you have to take an Emergency Moment to try and heal yourself a bit and remind yourself of a few things:

- Breathe all the way in and out, and keep doing that. Otherwise you start breathing like a small shrew in a trap.
- You have not killed anyone. You are not an arch criminal, not a murderer, not a terrorist. You are a good person who wants the best for others.
- You aren't being targeted for being rubbish at what you do – rather, it's because you're damned effective.
- Ordinary people are not fixated on your life or what is being said about you on Twitter. They are much more concerned about what's for tea or whether someone remembered to put the washing machine on.

When my boss called me in for a meeting, I was fairly sure it wasn't going to go well. I still wasn't certain that I would be fired because the whole thing was so damned ridiculous. Plus, my lovely radio show was one of the most listened-to commercial radio shows in my time slot. I was 'appointment listening', according to my boss, who had e-mailed me earlier in the week to say my recent shows were my best yet. So, there was hope.

On my way into the building a beautiful lady grabbed me to say how much she loved my radio show. Sometimes God really does give us a sign that there are bigger forces at work in our lives. The lady is Jewish – a woman who should have been most offended by me if the Left were to be believed – and she was my biggest supporter. I am super-blessed we have remained friends to this day.

Then I went into the room of pain. My boss was there with some other suit seated next to him, together with a few bits of paper that had dotted lines on them awaiting my signature – and I knew I was gone. Nothing mattered now; not one word from my mouth could make the slightest bit of difference. The decision had been made and I was being forced out.

I remember feeling cross. I was cross that these two men had ambushed me on my own, never offering me the chance to bring someone with me from Legal or someone I could ask for advice.

I was hurt by my boss, who knew how much I loved my show and my listeners, and how good I was at my job, but was unwilling to stick his neck out and defend me. I could barely look at him through my disgust.

I remembered the lady in reception telling me how much

she loved the show and how much my voice was needed.

I remember feeling so sad all of a sudden because I would miss my listeners and my show. Radio is the most authentic conversation you can have with your audience, and I probably hadn't appreciated just how much I love it.

And still, I managed to get out of the building and hold it together.

I put my little head up and my shoulders back and performed my Evita until I got out of there. I thanked reception, hugged security, and sashayed out.

I got around the corner and had to sit on a bench and eat chocolate until I stopped thinking I was going to pass out or be sick. That firing was by far the worst of my life – and a direct result of being good at what I do, having a political voice, and putting the fear of God into those in opposition to it. It descended on me like a concrete block dropped from a height. I was crushed.

Learnings

- Even if you don't realize you are powerful, at least recognize that you are well-paid and need to protect what you have. Make it someone's job to protect yours.
- Take a moment to appreciate how much you love what you do. Waiting until afterwards is wasted time. Be joyous in the moments.
- Cancel culture is now a worn playbook. Do not give those who wish to silence you or hurt you an open goal. I did, and I have to own that.
- You cannot mention any words used in association with

the Holocaust for any other purpose in life, not even if it's needlework or baking. There is an unwritten rule that any use of words at any time used in reference to the Holocaust means you are an anti-Semite – even if you just spent six months in Israel supporting Jewish works and you are on first-name terms with Bibi Netanyahu.

- Never enter a room with two men in suits and a few bits of paperwork. Turn on your heels and bring in reinforcements. Being ambushed is unacceptable. Men should have the decency to let you be prepared.
- If you were good at your job, one day you will feel better about being fired from it. I miss radio; I miss my listeners with all my heart; and I would love to do another show.

But there are crumbs of comfort in knowing that I was so good at something that I had to be shut down and that I still have that skill should I ever again be afforded the opportunity to use it.

If you ask me if I have any regrets in my life, it would be this: not being able to talk to my listeners and have them whisper me their secrets from their kitchen. It is a privilege, and one that is not lost on me.

CHAPTER 12

HELP,
I'M DEPRESSED

It really doesn't matter what age you are; sometimes we all reach a point where we flop into a chair and think: Christ-on-a-bike, I hate my life. We will call this the Chair of Despair.

We wonder what on earth is the point of all this? Why am I putting myself through this shit? And why doesn't everyone just FUCK RIGHT OFF?

Isn't it funny how we all live such separate and different lives and yet we all find ourselves in this exact position at certain points in our lives – unified by our absolute sense of being beaten by it all, flopped there in your work clothes or your pajamas wondering what your life is really all about.

In the Crazy Age of Covid many of us have felt that way more often than at any time before. Suddenly everyone has a view on your life and what you are supposed to be doing with it – particularly when it comes to the state injectable.

'Think of your family,' says the immunization nurse. 'Imagine how bad you would feel if you gave Covid to one of your elderly relatives.'

'It's selfish not to have the jab,' says a friend in your chat group, knowing your views but digging that dagger in regardless.

'Having the jab is the right thing to do for the country. You must think of others, not yourself,' says the Queen.

Coercive stuff is all about; we are surrounded by it – being told what to do and expected to comply, experiencing the worst of family guilt, and being ostracized from friendship groups if you fail to meet their implicit demands.

I left my own circle of friends on their WhatsApp chat a little over a year ago. I'm happy to say I didn't flounce off in a dramatic exit, rustling my flamenco skirts as I went. I didn't shout at any of them on the chat (caps lock on) or slam a door ('fuck you all!'). I just quietly took myself off. And, if you know me even just a little bit, you will know that 'quietly' and me aren't common bedfellows.

I was having a mini-rant back in 2020 about the madness of the fear being spread about Covid, and I saw the group reacting exactly as they would be expected to: scared shitless to go out or breathe in case they caught the killer virus. I tried, tactfully, to reassure them that the case numbers were low, the incidence of death was incredibly small, and there was no need to be afraid. The group leader – there is always one, even if without an official title with badge and desk – messaged me privately to ask if I was lying or at least saying this stuff just to make someone else feel better.

Her friends inside the NHS had basically passed along the absolute worst of the messaging they had been briefed with, and she had been plunged into a pit of panic. This is not her fault. Nor is it the fault of the NHS workers who were briefed to expect deaths unlike anything they had ever seen. Nor is it the fault of my friends in the group chat that they were terrified.

And, equally, I could have been completely wrong. But I could see the divisions happening.

When your chat group is not a group chatting

I was aware that multiple groupschat groups were now operating – one with the whole group, one with the whole group minus the cancer sufferer, one with the group minus 'new friends', a group minus Hopkins? Who knows? And none of that matters either; that is personal choice.

What sort of friendship group are we if we can't all be in it together? Why are some things okay to say and others not? And who gets to be the policeman of all that?

I was reminded of my other life on Twitter, where the list of things you could say was getting smaller and smaller, and how I was now watching that situation mutate over into my most private life with the group that I trusted to know the real me. It felt like the end of a road.

So I walked away, quietly, and have not returned. I'd like to return one day, and I miss having those friends in my life. I miss the easy laughter of being all together and of belonging, accumulated over years and years. I miss having those friends in my life and I miss being in theirs.

I also feel guilty that many of them are going through hard things – their parents also – and I am not there to at least offer some words of support. I still have those words; I still mean those words; and I wish them every lucky thing, even if I am not expressing it on a group chat. I am still the same me and I want the best for all of them.

But I know me. There is no space in my friendship group for thoughts like mine. And, if I am not very careful, I will keep fighting for my views to be accepted – something I have never wanted to bring into my most private world.

I share all of this because I know this is how many people feel, not only being ostracized in the grocery line or trying to get on board a plane but also surrounded by judgmental friends who seem to be certain their opinion is right and yours is wrong. The only explanation my friend had for my views differing so fundamentally from hers is that I must be lying.

We have found ourselves isolated from the very people we used to be closest to, and it's a perfectly horrible thing that has been done to the most important relationships in our lives. These relationships will have to be rebuilt in time. Mine will, too, but trying to rebuild against a backdrop of lockdown, guilt, blame, and unkindness would be before its time.

I also share these private stories of separation from my friends because, while my own experience happened during Covid and because of CORONA HYSTERIA, it is the same experience that others feel in everyday life when they are made to feel wrong or insignificant or are left out of their friendship groups. At some point you find yourself flopped in the chair in your kitchen wondering, how the hell did I end up all alone like this?

I receive letters every day from family members who have been excluded from their closest family. Irish friends of mine were just disinvited from a family funeral because they have not had the vaccine. Another lady has been told she can't come to the family dinner when her mother visits from Spain because she is the only one who hasn't had the jab. This is utter insanity.

A grown man, twenty years a Marine fighting for his son's

future, wept on my shoulder in Arizona – because his son no longer wants to be part of his life. Another lady, and a great one, told me quietly in her car that her two grown daughters refuse to speak to her until she apoloigses for what she has said about the vaccine and accept Biden is President.

Humanity has lost its tiny mind.

It isn't just Covid. Women are particularly vulnerable to the power of the group and what it means to be excluded from it. Motherhood is the first bitter taste of this, where there is a right way and a wrong way to parent – where you are a good mother if you do this but a bad mother if you don't. And chat groups led by Perfect Priscilla, who shares pictures of the fruit kebabs and salad landscapes she has made for her three-year-old triplets, all terribly good-looking and dressed in Kate-Middleton-inspired smocks.

At 40 or 50 many of us are sandwiched at both ends of our life: caring for elderly parents and trying to be a decent parent ourselves – and trying to find some energy left over to be a wife. Throw in a job, the housework, and the odd disaster, and it's little wonder you find yourself in the Chair of Despair, wondering how you became so trapped by it all and how it can be humanly possible for one woman to wind up being emotionally responsible for so many things.

Sometimes you look at a picture of an easy, breezy, young thing in a bikini busying herself with a fleet or TikTok dance routine, and imagine, for a moment, how glorious it would be to have such an empty head and for the shape of your eyebrows to be your greatest challenge and achievement.

I have these moments often, mostly when I can hear the

washing machine beeping that its work is done but it seems everyone else has gone deaf. Or I am replacing the tenth toilet roll of the day, or trying to clear the shoe pile from the mat because the dang front door won't even open.

It's not your father's heart attack that causes you to blow your top, or the multiple-car pile-up you were involved in. It is the insanely small stuff that is the final grain of sand that brings your whole castle crumbling down.

Young people are not immune from the Chair of Despair; in fact, some have spent more time in it than out.

One thing is certain: phones have screwed the young. Would I have done half the stuff I did in my earlier life in the age of the chuffing iPhone? I know I would not. I was blessed to grow up in an age of anonymity.

I fear that, by the age of ten or eleven (perhaps even younger?), children with a phone or gadget will have had more unkind words directed at them – in writing – than anyone my age ever experienced in the whole of their young lives.

Freaks that run places like Google and Facebook might try to tell us that, 'thanks to social media', we are more connected than at any time in history. I would argue social isolation and ostracism in the age of social media is more acute than at any time in history too, particularly if you are under 30 years old.

Imagine writing down something horribly unkind about your own child, something truly terrible – and then putting it in his or her hands and watching them read it. You simply wouldn't do it, couldn't do it. But this is the reality of social media. This is the magnitude of the monster that adults have created.

One thing all of us can agree on is that online life is not easier than real life. I'd argue it's harder because it separates us from real life and the things that make us feel better.

Sometimes I feel like I am on dementia-repeat mode when I tell young people or adults to 'step away from the noise' by taking a break from social media. I am also certain that the intervention of my husband Mark in helping me to do just that has been the only thing that has saved me from myself and, at times, the mob.

That's the thing about phones, of course, or gadgets.

In real life the jibes of playground bullies and groups of kids in the street stay outside. They might be pretty damned uncomfortable; I can remember the sticky agony of walking past the kids from the state school all dressed up in my uniform, a kilt and blazer, and being taunted as a posh twat. I remember the teeth-itching agony of being laughed at by lads in a line for the bar, hearing myself being called 'Concorde' because of my big nose. You know the way sweat prickles on you when you are acutely ashamed? I have a memory of that stinging rash even now.

But somehow, once I was home or around friends, it all got left behind or, at least, put off until tomorrow. We used to be able to suspend everything else when we stepped inside our front door; we were able to leave the world and any unkindness outside.

But phones don't get left behind. Young people invite the monster to come inside with them, bring it into their bedrooms. Many of us place the monster right next to our pillow, buzzing and beeping whenever it wants our attention, making sure we don't take a break away to sleep.

It becomes almost impossible to put down, so much so that you start to reason with your own brain: 'Right, one more message, or one last comment, then I am turning this thing off.' Except that you can't or don't or won't.

And the more you start to read stuff that upsets you, the more you are drawn into it. It's like heroin for the eyeballs – chasing the dragon for hurt even as you feel it biting you, until eventually, finally you look up and realize your neck is stiff and two hours have just disappeared, all making you feel worse, less, or more horrible than you did before.

The phrase 'doom-scrolling' has come into use, which is a perfect way to describe my own teenage daughter and the weird way she can pass an entire evening with her phone not more than half an arm's length from her face, constantly scrolling and scrolling and scrolling.

Not all of it is doom, to be sure. Much more of it is girls plucking their eyebrows, putting on eye makeup, doing ridiculous dance routines to the camera in their own bathrooms while trying to look hot, or pretending to be natural with their good-looking boyfriends while trying to look hot.

I shouldn't be unkind. There have been moments when I have laughed along as well. The videos of dogs narrating their own thoughts using automated voice software are hilarious, but that hardly puts me up with some of the great thinkers of our time. Social media is a sinkhole that will suck you in, gobble you up, and cause you to disappear forever in a pit without end, if you let it.

The most important rule for dealing with social media itself is knowing it is a nasty bastard. Whatever app it is, whatever platform, whatever you do to feed it – it is taking from you. The more time you can TAKE BACK from social media, the stronger you will become.

The young have not yet started to LIVE their lives, and yet already they face more setbacks and sinkholes than most of us ever did.

In this age of mass compliance and groupthink, some have taken an alternative route to avoiding feeling the hurt of being left out and have done a full about-face on it. Instead of trying to be part of the group and fit in, they aim to be as odd as possible to demonstrate they have no intention of conforming to anything, especially not to how they think they are wanted to feel. I know a gentleman who got his entire body covered in tattoos and then began the process of tattooing his own eyeballs; at the very least, he has shunned the notion of fitting in.

Others seem happy to cut off their own genitals and identify as a wombat if it elevates them from the crowd. There are women prepared to make themselves as ugly as it is possible to be, à la Lena Dunham, to prove that the crowd is not for them. These individuals are the exception, not the rule, and even the transgendered, bisexual vegan with a black boyfriend ends up being surrounded by others eventually. I can remember when being a lesbian was still considered pretty punk rock.

I think there is a middle ground.

It cannot be about absorbing endless hurt when you feel excluded or overlooked, and it is certainly not about trying to stand out like a butch lesbian growing her armpit hair and basket-weaving it into a sign that says 'FUCK YOU!'

I suspect trying to deal with the Chair of Despair isn't really about a group, or Covid, or your family, or work, or lack of it.

I think it might actually be trying to be the most comfortable version of yourself, whatever that may be – like being in your pajamas when you get home from work or your home clothes on a weekend. Being comfy is actually a very aspirational thing; Lovely Mark would call it 'contented'. I think contentment is aspirational, and yet no one talks of it in this way.

The other night I met a young man who likes to go on cruise ships alone. He likes the lifestyle, he likes the gambling machines, and he enjoys escaping alone this way. I think it is a remarkable sign of personal contentment, to be able to spend time alone with yourself this way.

Getting out of the Chair of Despair and getting comfy with yourself isn't a destination or an endpoint.

Getting comfy is more like a long walk with yourself – it just keeps going. The more you walk with yourself, the more comfy you are aiming to get. It helps to explain why 80-year-olds can be so much fun to be around – the lively ones with all of their faculties intact, not the sadly demented ones who smell vaguely of piss and don't know their own names.

You don't have to be old to be comfy with yourself. I have met lovely 30- and 40-year-olds who have achieved this to near-perfection. One picks grapes for a living; the other helps women in a refuge and makes her own clothes; another has horses, and they are her life.

You could argue they are avoiding the difficult bits – demanding jobs, complicated families, front-facing jobs – and I think there is truth in that. But you know, the things they all share in common are that they are not in the least bit bothered by being online (two don't have smartphones), and they aren't geared into the usual metrics of success (job, house, car, family, friends). They have their own measures in their lives, and none of these include follower numbers or messages on a chat group. They are comfy as they walk and will only get comfier. Your way to feeling better is to imagine yourself walking behind them, as if along a shoreline on a beach. They may be way off in the distance, like little dots in the sun, and you may feel like you are treading on eggshells or walking on glass, but you are on the path to being comfy.

Perhaps none of us is meant to fit in at all; we are just meant to be as comfy as we can possibly be, even if that means letting go of some of the stuff we once imagined was so important to our success.

The Chair of Despair Learnings

- Feeling left out really hurts. Before you can fix it, you have to acknowledge it. There is no point in trying to be brave or cool about it.

- Being told to 'forget about it' or 'don't think about it; you have plenty of other friends' or 'forget the old cow; she's not worth it' will not help at all. It is the equivalent of having a kitchen knife in your eyeball and being told to blink as normal.

- You need to process what it is that actually hurts. What it is that's really upsetting you. Keep asking 'so what?' until you get to the truth of the thing. 'I was left out of the chat.' So what? 'So, my mates deliberately left me out.' So what? And so on until you get to the real reason why you are hurt.

- No matter how humiliating the truth sounds, you are going to need to share it (possibly with a piece of paper), think about how to get rid of it, and ask for help in doing that. Once you have begun that process of dealing with the hurt, you can imagine putting it into a box, putting the box on the shelf, and making a pact with yourself to leave it there.

- From now on, you have to try not to go back to the 'so whats'. If you do want to go back, you have to get the box, think about what you are doing to fix the problem, and re-imagine putting that into the box.

- We have to own our problems. It is too easy to imagine our happiness is dependent on the love of many or the opinions of others, and then blame them when we feel unhappy. If you feel unhappy, you are the only one with the power to change that; even if it needs the help of someone else, you own 'unhappy' and 'happy'.

- Perspective can really lend a hand. You feel stupid because you know that what is upsetting you is silly. Don't feel stupid! If it is silly, be glad. You can find a way around it, and you will.

- Be discerning. It's great to be able to share stuff, but do it to help yourself feel comfortable. Don't share yourself with those who use it as fuel in their tank or collateral with the group, where gossip is like cash.

- What do you really want to do? If you had no commitments, there was no one around, and you weren't worried about what anyone thought of you, what would you do? How can you do more of that thing in your life? (If your answer to the first question is 'take drugs, sleep with a stranger, and don't wake up for two days', you may be avoiding your issues as opposed to working through them. This is okay, as long as you are clear.)

- See yourself on a walk to being comfy with yourself. It is hard to achieve as a teenager, tricky as a 20-year-old, and confusing at 30 years of age, but it gets easier and easier as you walk. Others in front of you have shown that it can be done.

- Kindness is out there in surprising places. So often in my life when I have been plummeting face first towards the ground, the unexpected kindess has come from surprising places to break my fall. True friendship might be quietly waiting for you off to the side.

- Fuel up on the good stuff for your walk. Make yourself remember all the great things in your life, things that have gone well, really kind things you have done for someone else. Kindness multiplies; I am certain of it. If we spent half as much time remembering the good things about ourselves as we do persecuting the minutes of half-meant nothings, we'd be the Kings and Queens of Comfy.

Go do good things. You are not left out. You are Kings and Queens of Comfy. If you are true to yourself, and only want the best for others, walk forwards with your head held high. You are braver than you know.

CHAPTER 13

HELP,
I CAN'T GO ON

There are times in life when you ask, 'What the hell did I ever do to deserve this?'

I was awarded the CUNT award – yes, you read that correctly, CUNT; as in the most foul word in the whole of the human language – and was duped into travelling to Prague to give an acceptance speech and collect the award in person.

A famous You-Tuber set the whole prank up, hooked me in via e-mail, hired a venue, flew me in, hired a team of actors to play the part of the crowd, briefed hotel staff and others to be in on the prank, and filmed the whole thing.

The footage has been viewed over 12 million times; my humiliation at the hands of these gentlemen is one of the most viewed clips on YouTube in recent years. It is red meat to the salivating mob of wolves who despite me, my success, my views – or indeed, all three.

You might wonder how the hell this happened. You might wonder just how stupid (vain / dumb / naïve / idiotic) I had to be for them to pull this off.

I have been seated at a very private dinner and asked by another woman, 'How on earth could you be so stupid?' as a way to belittle me in the eyes of the influential people present at the table.

You might wonder why the hell I am writing about it here (when this is my own book) and reliving my own crucifixion. It's not how most middle-aged menopausal women want to spend their time, and I have to say, I have thought about deleting this whole chapter on more than one occasion. 'Let's just not go there,' I have consoled myself.

Except, of course, that is the opposite of the advice I am trying to dispense here in HELP! It is the very opposite of what I am asking you to do. I am asking you to be completely honest about how you really feel about the things that are hurting you the most.

And if I am asking it of you, then I have to do it too. Although I am sure that most of you will not have received a CUNT award in person, there are moments in most lives that are relatable – particularly if you have been humiliated in front of your friends. This moment was the same gut punch I felt when I learned my husband was leaving me for the secretary and had been sleeping with her all the time I had been pregnant – and everyone else knew about it but me.

I also hope that, by sharing this horrific story, you will see that, through it all, we can prevail. It is not that your humiliation is less than mine; it is never smart to imagine that you set the bar for how terrible things can be, so that others must appreciate that their suffering is always less. That is nonsense.

We have all been humiliated, and it is always as horrific for each one of us. But, by setting out what you really feel and applying a structure of steel to your thinking, you can start to feel better. I promise. So, here goes.

I picked up my phone, read the text message, and felt my heart crush in its little cage.

'Given that you have been kicked off Twitter, I thought I had better tell you in person. You flew to Prague for no reason – there was no real award. You accepted a CUNT Award. Full video posting soon.'

Some of you will know the feeling.

I mean, not that you will have been stitched up and received a CUNT Award in front of three million viewers on YouTube – that's just in my crazy world – but you will know that weird, icy-cold feeling you get when you hear horrible news and the blood falls out of your head because your heart demands all of it just to keep beating.

Things go black and white. You have to sit down. You think you might be sick.

That was me.

I had been flown to Prague to be given the CUNT Award, had given a speech to accept it, allowed the whole thing to be filmed, and even signed the release papers for my stupidity to be published to the world. And, worst of all, I was so knackered and invested in the reason I thought I was there that I didn't question a thing. I thought I was going to show my love and support for the white farmers of South Africa – picking up the Campaign to Unify the Nation Award trophy in the process. I was wrong.

It had not been an easy weekend.

I had just returned home from a two-month tour of America – rallying patriots behind President Trump and helping lift our side. I had been on the road for six weeks and had no body clock left to speak of. My trip to Prague to 'support white farmers' was the last thing I did before finally flying home, absolutely battered, and just wanting to lie in a dark room and sleep.

At the same time, I was being given a world-class pummeling by the Twitter mob, as I had finally been removed from the site (courtesy of a personal intervention by Rachel Riley and a Muslim-funded pressure group), and Muslims and leftists were rejoicing as if they had just been told that all Brexit and Trump supporters were being sent to concentration camps.

And now this – the CUNT award.

I had been taken for a fool; I had been made to look like an idiot. I was the butt of a huge joke that was about to explode across the internet. Worse still, right up until that moment, I genuinely thought I had done something kind for my friends in South Africa – but the opposite was true.

Josh Pieters is South African. He presented himself as a South African farmer, helping run a support group for farmers being butchered on their land. He knew I had made a documentary on the subject; he knew my whole heart was with these people. He used it well. I will do anything for South Africans – and I think it overrode any suspicion on my part that I was being taken for a fool.

As rough days go, I think I was right up there with Harvey Weinstein standing in court hearing his genitals being described as weirdly deformed. There are times in this exposed life of mine when I do just want to lie down on the cold grass outside my home and ask the ground to give way and swallow me up. I want to find complete darkness, and for the soil to fill up my ears and shut out the noise in my head.

There are times when I am not certain I will make it.

Perhaps you have seen an animal injured on the roadside or a little mouse caught by a cat, and watched its breathing get fast and shallow, gasping at the periphery of life to try to re-inflate itself and keep its heart beating. That's exactly what this feels like: gasping at the periphery of life as you are being crushed by the weight of the hurt of it all.

I have always said the mob will not stop until you swing from a tree. And it is perfectly true in my life.

It is perfectly clear that those who wish to silence you will not stop until you are ended. It is clear that other, darker forces are prepared to fund these attacks on you, pushing you to the very edge of life, and that your death is the only thing that will satiate them. It is true that, even after your death, they would lust for more – showing your kids they were celebrating, or retweeting the purchase of 'the witch is dead' so it tops the charts in order that your family feel mocked in their pain.

This is the reality of being me. This is the reality of standing up for what you believe in – as opposed to what you are allowed to think.

Caroline Flack

Not long after the horrible suicide of the brilliant, effervescent Caroline Flack, a British media personality and beautiful soul, the hashtag #BeKind made the rounds.

Caroline took her own life when allegations that she had physically assaulted her boyfriend made headline news, together with some pretty grim private photographs allegedly of the scene.

There was a bed, a bloodied lampshade, and claims of an attack by Caroline on her boyfriend in the middle of the night. The mob couldn't get enough of it. Women resented her success; many were jealous of her magic; legions wanted to be her but couldn't – while others just saw a vehicle for their own crusade, or were pulled in out of pure boredom or spite.

Her works cancelled her: she lost her role presenting on Love Island and she was cast out as a leper. I couldn't hear a single voice trying to defend her.

She will have found it unbearable. I know this feeling. It is like being crushed, the way bodies are crushed when air pressure is lost.

The #BeKind hashtag was too late for Caroline because the mob came for her and claimed her heart. Even those who knew they had played a part in her death jumped on the bandwagon and tweeted the #BeKind hashtag, hoping to cleanse themselves of culpability.

But even those empty platitudes and hashtags do not extend to someone who holds a different political opinion. Because I support Trump and Brexit and believe that Brits should be put first above all others in the UK, I am fair game, as are so many of my allies on the road.

I am amazed that Justice Brett Kavanaugh did not end his own life when his family became the target of a heinous witch-hunt aimed at derailing his nomination to the U.S. Supreme Court. I look at the face of that man, and I see he came mighty close.

Once you reach the point where you believe there is no way

out, no way to stop it, no way to protect your family from it, the logical, rational argument is for you to end your own life in the hope that all of the bad things will end with you, too. You want to free those whom you care about, and one selfless act would seem to be the key to this freedom. I have re-run that argument many times; I understand it.

You will understand this, too, if you have ever truly considered suicide. You will understand it is not a selfish act but a selfless one, aimed at trying to protect others from the venom that seems to surround you.

I understand Caroline Flack, in the eye of her own media storm, making her last climb to hang herself from the bannisters in her own home and kicking the chair away. I can almost feel her foot reaching out to end it. She had been left alone by her minder for five minutes; she knew she only had five minutes to make it all stop. She took her chance.

There are times when I want it all to go away so badly, and I know with certainty that the only way to make it go away is to make myself go away too. If you have walked this path, you will understand – and you have my whole heart in your support.

In these moments, I want the darkness to close over me and the noise to be silenced and not to have to face any of it anymore. I have always understood why people drown themselves for this very reason; it is a physical articulation of how you feel on the inside, when you just want it all to go away and find peace under the water.

I have always had huge admiration for those who down a bottle of whiskey (single malt, obviously), leave their clothes folded neatly in a pile on the sand, and walk naked into the sea, never to return. While many people talk of suicide as being a coward's way out, I see so much power in this solitary act. The folded clothes are part of signaling to others that you were in control of your thoughts and actions right up until the end. You made a rational choice not to continue, and you did it neatly.

I am not encouraging this behavior; I repeat, I am NOT encouraging this behavior or celebrating it. I am not one of those freaks online who goads someone else to their end. But – I understand it, and I see power in personal choice. And I believe that life is only a gift if you also keep the power to take it away.

On days like this day, knackered, the target of the mob online, the victim of a hoax, your humiliation about to be thrown as red meat into the Coliseum of Hate, you gain real clarity about what it is like to be truly alone.

It's lonely out front

There is incredible clarity in this loneliness, too.

It is a bit like being inside of a Plexiglas box, or one of those giant inflatable balls that people roll about in, only a lot less fun. You can see other people, see your friends on the outside going along as normal, but nothing they say reaches you. No one can really understand this because they aren't in the crosshairs, and the blunt truth is that, if any of this happened to them – even a sniff of it – they would fold in an instant. It's not normal to withstand this kind of pressure. It's an accumulative thing – like a marathon runner, you have to put in the mileage to withstand this level of pain.

I say this without self-pity.

In the normal world, when there is the mildest issue on Facebook or in a WhatsApp group – for example, someone leaves a slightly unkind comment or appears to make a snarky remark – it often results in a huge meltdown, tears, histrionics, and someone being blocked or people not speaking. All of that happens because of a small scrap between a handful of people within your personal space.

Now scale this up. Take a small WhatsApp falling-out and multiply it by a million, apply a loudspeaker, paint it orange, stick your own name all over it, and have 12 million people laughing at a picture of you holding a CUNT Award.

Everything is amplified until the noise is screaming in your face like a jet engine, frying your eyeballs, scalding and peeling your skin off. There is just noise and pain.

How to help

It is not easy to help someone who has made a rational decision to end their own life. It is not easy to help someone struggling, or in pain, or feeling the only way to find peace is to end it all.

I can tell you what not to say:

- 'You will get over this; you've had worse'
  This is one of the most unkind things I hear. It offers zero understanding of where your head is, and is laced with deliberate unkindness. It says, 'With all of the shit you have kicked up in your shitty life, you have done shittier things than this. Eat shit!' It is the opposite of help. This person has no understanding of what you are going through but is

apoplectic if their cleaning lady doesn't show up when she is supposed to.

- 'What have you gone and said now?'
This is right up there with major-league asshole things to say. It assumes that all of this crap is always your fault, and that the major pile-on being coordinated by those who wish to silence you is a reaction to something you have done. It is trite and trivial, and shows they don't at all understand what you stand for, why it matters, or why this hurts. Silence is the only way to deal with this person.

- 'It's water off a duck's back with you, isn't it?'
This doesn't come close to support. It is the offer of aspirin when what you need is life support. It's not even a blanket, soft and comforting somehow; it's hard, unfeeling, and leaves you wondering whether these people really know you at all. Or, at least, it makes you want to blame your friends alongside the mob online, given that they are supposed to know you but really don't seem to get it at all.

The noise of the mob pile-on and unkindness on this scale sometimes make you want others to have a 10-second blast of it, just to power-wash your world into their life for a moment – as if you had your fingertips around the volume dial of their life and you could suddenly whack it up to full, just for a brief moment, so they could at least start to connect with the noise and what it feels like when darkness descends.

These are bitter and spiteful thoughts; they are unkind and vindictive. I am ashamed of thinking them.

But help and hope are out there.

There are possibly five people I trust to understand and help get me through these moments. All have had elements of what happens to me happen to them, and all are able to reach through the Plexiglas separating me from normal people and offer me a hand of support.

They whisper quietly in my ear that they are sorry for what I am going through. They remind me that I am a good person, I am trying to do the right thing. They reassure me that this will pass and tell me they are there if I need them.

I have only one phrase I use to try to signal to those close enough to understand that I am suffering: 'This is dark.' I mean this is near the edge of what I can take; the darkness is just at my fingertips, as is the soil I want to close over me, or the water that could fill my ears and make the noise go away. Others who have been pushed to the edge of the abyss know what 'this is dark' means: 'I think I am going to break.'

Help seldom comes from those closest to home or friends you made in school. Help probably won't come from the people you invited to your wedding or included in your most private moments. My hope and help are in Ireland, New York City, Virginia, the southernmost tip of the UK, and the chilly cold of Denver, Colorado, and Minnesota. My help will see themselves located here and know their place in my heart.

When I am in my darkest place, there are people out there who know firsthand that the only way to help is to pull me through it. But not with sympathy or jokes, or by trying to get me to laugh at myself. They literally pull me through this bit of my life with kindness and concern. It is as if they tie a rope around me; in my mind, it is a big, chunky rope, like the ones on fishing boats, all worn, bleached, and impossible to lift alone, the sort that can hold a ship in stormy seas, anchor it solid in uncertainty. The rope goes around my waist and they knot it, telling me that it is there, fixed in place, and they now have me. 'We gotcha, we gotcha,' they say, cutting me free from the wreckage of this car crash, even if it was of my own making.

And, for the first time, I find I can let go a bit, suddenly aware of the tense thing in my stomach trying to keep me upright and the muscles in my back and neck straining to hold me together.

Now that the rope is around me, it's okay to let go of trying to be in control. Their rope says I can't trip, can't accidentally leave, and cannot be carried off by a wave of sadness. I can feel it tugging at my back. And my trusted friends remind me that, although this is just awful, it will pass.

'This too shall pass' was said to me by my radio-show producer as we sat in the studio in London when yet another scandal was engulfing my life. Funnily enough, I can remember the light in the room, the desk we were sitting at, the feel of the newspapers on my fingers, the time of day, and the laughter we later shared. Her words are locked into my head alongside all the memories of that moment.

There is such power in those words. I have no idea why, but it is a mantra for enduring whatever pain I am in. 'This too shall pass.'

These words are a reminder that you have endured before and you will do so again. More than that: there is reason for what you do; it is not for nothing that this is hard.

This is a kind of holding pattern. All you have to do is hold on – to the handful of people you can count on, to the sturdy rope they have tied around your waist – and to breathe fresh air in big gulps like a thirsty sailor who has been marooned before. Because hours turn to days, and the days pass to a point where, finally, one night you have a good sleep – one where your head doesn't hurt, your teeth aren't clenched, and you can lift your head a little bit.

And then the kindness of strangers kicks in, messages from those you don't know telling you they are there for you, cheering you on. It is an amazing thing that a stranger will take the time and make the effort to let you know that what's happened is bloody awful and they are sorry. It is these messages from strangers that start to give you strength to emerge from the holding pattern into a place where you start to breathe in whole breaths that go all the way in and all the way out.

Perhaps you can finally start to talk about how you are feeling and why it was so hurtful; maybe you feel able to go out and walk down the street, realizing that not everyone you see is pointing at you.

You could be reading all of this thinking, 'What a massive overreaction to a bit of media nonsense,' or recalling the time when you were told you had cancer or that you had failed to get the job you desperately needed – real things that really mattered to your life. I see and respect your perspective.

I have also come to realize that no one owns the rights to how others feel. No one sets the metric for pain. What happens in your life is the only barometer you have and, if you are lucky, someone else out there in the universe will understand what you are going through, has come close to it themselves, and will know the right words that will help you hold on long enough to see the light. I have been blessed to have had those people cross my path, and they are still crossing it now.

I once had very severe surgery to remove a tumor from my brain. My skull was sawed open from ear to ear, sixty-four staples were implanted across my head, and I spent three months in a London hospital. I know what physical hurt is. But that still does not make me the arbiter of pain or serve to dismiss the suffering of others as lesser than my own. When I ask how someone is, and they tell me about their terrible sore throat, I still care for them in that moment; I do not take their throat and measure it against my greatest pain and reject it as trifling.

I think the same is true for those who end up in a dark place and consider ending their life as a way out. You cannot pretend to know their path, nor does comparing it with your own ever help. None of us owns the metric for suffering. The only thing you can do is throw out a rope, tie it around their waist, and take the strain for them, to stop them from accidentally falling. You can remind them softly that this will pass and try to keep them holding on until it does. No one knows how long the storm will blow for in their own lives, and you cannot see the horizon clearly until it does. You need to get them into a holding pattern that they can sustain until the storm passes. Because I can tell you this for certain: the sun does come out again. The light does come and the darkness recedes.

I have walked away from friends who seem to use my life as entertainment for their own or as collateral for their WhatsApp chats, feigning sympathy but enjoying my hurt. And I feel happier for it. I miss the friends I thought I had, but I am not entirely sure if what I thought I had was all that honest in the end. 'Friend' is an overused term; it hides all manner of hurts and sins.

And so I survived accepting the CUNT Award and being thrown off Twitter to live another day. I know that those who wish to silence me will not stop until I am swinging from a tree. I sometimes wonder who will win, but I do not fear them, and I do not fear the end.

I walk towards it. I know the strongest of us are tested in the hottest fires, and I am not scared of the furnace.

I have endured. I want to help others endure as I have done. My children already know the epitaph I want leaned against my final tree: 'Katie Hopkins – she died standing up.'

Postscript

Sitting on a bench and minding my own business in London, guess who comes up to say hello? Josh Pieters, the gentleman who orchestrated the CUNT Award and my absolute humiliation in front of about 12 million people.

He smiled, joking that I shouldn't worry because he wasn't secretly filming me, not today at least.

Every last bit of me wanted to claw at his skin, bite through his neck, and end him, yelling, 'You evil little bastard, you posh, privileged dickhead, you hurt me, you hurt the things I care about, you used the people I love. You made me feel sick about my own stupidity; you took my kindness and made it something horrid. And you knew, you know, you have seen how I am.

'All I wanted to do was go home and see my family, but I came for you because you said it was for the white farmers. And you lied and are a wretched, horrible person. What the fuck do you think that does to a woman? You filmed me in the streets when I thought I was alone. I am a mum with kids who need me, you privileged little shit, and you used my kindness and made it hurt.'

My better self arrived, not a moment too soon. (I imagine my better self in running shoes with neatly shaved legs, cute hair, and a controlled level of body fat – but that's a whole other issue.)

'I really don't want to speak to you,' I managed, despite my throat raging at the tears I would not allow to come.

He seemed disappointed. 'Not at all? There is nothing that you want to say to me? Did you not think it funny, not even a little bit?'

I just looked at him, a scruffy boy in yesterday's t-shirt. He looked different than I remembered, without his paid goons around him – tired, unshaven, not showered, buying his sad little breakfast-for-one from a lonely Waitrose beneath his posh little flat that was bought with daddy's money.

Without my words, he had nothing. Without my anger, he was empty-handed. He walked away, and I felt somehow more peace.

I genuinely think he believed I would laugh a little, call him a few names, give him some classic lines to be able to share as swag with his fawning admirers. With nothing, that's exactly what he had.

I am grateful to my mouth for defying my head and refusing to say all of the stuff I was desperate to yell. He still has no idea about the impact of what he did. His followers all think he is a superstar; my haters love that footage more than having sex with themselves – which they do often. And I cannot control any of that.

It is at these moments the wisdom of India – my child who was not normal enough to be born – is at its most brilliant.

When everything was crashing down and I tried to explain to her that 'Mummy was tricked by a man into travelling to Prague, doing a speech, and picking up an award so they could make Mummy look stupid in front of everyone,' she thought for a moment and said, 'Well, that is not very nice.' Windy does turn understatement into an art form. She then proceeded to give me something she has seen other people do with their arms and call 'a hug'. She has seen this used to make people feel better, so she copied the idea.

With Windy, it's an awkward physical moment, like wrapping a circle up in a triangle – all elbows and chin – but it's just the loveliest thing she is trying to show. And, with a few simple questions, she put my world back on its axis again:

Q: Did you do what you said you would do?

A: Yes.

Q: Were you nice to the people you met?

A: Yes.

Q: Did you get paid?

A: Well, yes, they covered my expenses. I turned up early, gave a speech I liked, was kind to the waiters and waitresses and everyone in the room, and wrote a thank-you note to the 'organizer' afterwards. I even offered to visit the elderly father figure I was told was poorly (all a lie). So, yes, I did the right thing.

India: Then, what's the big deal, Mum? You did everything you said you would do. You were nice to the people who worked hard. And you have done nothing wrong.

We all need an India. We all need to remember that this too shall pass.

Lessons from the CUNT Award

- When you are the target of the online mob, you just want to find a way to make the noise stop. Sometimes you think the only way to make the noise stop is to end yourself. This is understandable, but it is a short-term view.
- Friends might not be the ones to help you when you are facing down the darkness. Some people that you call 'friends' will be enjoying your suffering. These people are not friends. They feel better when you feel worse.
- Strangers who understand will help you. They will get you to a safe place where you can hold on. They will put a rope around your waist; all you have to do is to cling on.
- This too shall pass. Say it over and over; it has special powers.
- One day, you will feel strong enough to lift your head up again and see that you have endured and are stronger because of it.
- You can only control the things you have responsibility for; you cannot control the actions of others. Josh Pieters is accountable for what he did and, undoubtedly, he thinks he did something terrific. I hope perhaps he reads this one day and takes the time to understand I am not a monster and that he humiliated me – a fairly ordinary woman, a mother

like any other, and a proud supporter of the white farmers of South Africa.

- I have to be accountable for what I did and all that I have done. I am proud of the speech I gave and the bravery of the South African farmers whom I love.
- I am certain that, if you asked any of the wait staff in that hotel – or even the actors paid by Josh Pieters to humiliate me – they would only have kind words to say about me. I suspect some of them even felt badly for participating in my humiliation. I don't hold any ill will toward them, or to the boy responsible for all of this. And perhaps that is enough.

CHAPTER 14

HELP, I'M DYING

Let's get a few things said upfront and without apology about cancer, terminal illness, and death. I will not be holding back and want to give you, the reader, fair warning. If you are incredibly hung over or are in the middle of a row with your spouse, now may not be the time to have this thrust in your face; come back to this chapter when you are feeling ready.

Just because you have been diagnosed with cancer does not mean you have a terminal illness or that you are going to die. While these things go without saying, sometimes we need to be reminded of the obvious and reassured that the evil voices in our head are often wrong.

My grandfather is testament to the cancer-doesn't-mean-death thing. Diagnosed with prostate cancer almost before I was born, and looking for a long while as if he would outlive me, he made it to 99 years old. And it wasn't the cancer that got him in the end, but rather old age; it was just time for him to take a well-earned rest.

We understand that the Big C and Death are two different things. But for those of us who have sat in a brightly lit room with their consultant and a box of tissues and had The

Conversation, it is high time we talk about it, bollocks out, boobs out, and nothing left inside. Being diagnosed with cancer does inevitably make you think you might die, and there is no point in hiding from that. A terminal diagnosis does put you on death row medically, with specific, real thoughts that we don't talk enough about. Vomiting up what I think about this stuff might have two effects: (a) make you incredibly glad you don't think like me and remind you that, in relative terms, you are still sane, or (b) make you realize you are not alone with dark and difficult thoughts and that, when you actually talk them out, they seem a whole lot less frightening. Talking about terminal illness is the only way to handle it, and the more we practice talking about it, the better we get. Plus, if you really only have a few months left, you don't have time to waste feeling trapped with your own thoughts.

Don't be alarmed. This won't be the trite crap you hear from those who aren't really connecting to their words; this isn't the awkwardly upbeat crap you get from your neighbor who ends every conversation with 'We all die one day!' and thinks he is being helpful. Yes, neighbor, we do, but if you had your sell-by-date written on the inside of your eyelids at night when the rest of the world was sleeping soundly, you might not be so friggin' anally retentive about your lawn.

There will be no niceties here, no gently reassuring phrases spewed out by people who have never felt the fear themselves, only straight talk learned from my own brush with being terminal, in the hope that we can chat about it together whenever you feel you need a friend.

Strangely, my brush with being terminal was not because

of the Big C. 'Strangely' because, given my family history, it feels almost inevitable and, as I am only 46 years old, perfectly possible that cancer will come into my life at some point, like some uninvited guest with halitosis, and sweep me away.

One in six people will get cancer in their lifetime, which means that, in an average family of eight or twelve people, there are a couple you're going to know – and hence the bloody cruelty of someone's wife and mother having it at the same time. I wonder how some families manage to endure what they do, but they say it is because there is no choice: their only option is to endure.

My family is no exception. Funnily – or more aptly, macabrely – nearly a whole person could be made out of all the bits that my family has had chopped off because of cancer. A whole person made out of the Hopkins Cancerous Bits.

My lovely mum had one boob completely removed at the age of 34; my grandad had most of his ear cut off from skin cancer; my grandma had a double mastectomy; and my father has had enough skin cut off his head to cover a small person. I have had two moles removed, and my sister three, although I don't think our cancer-monster would thank us for adding moles just for effect.

Admittedly, we are missing a few important bits for an actual functioning human body, but if we add the amputations unrelated to cancer (both my Nan's legs and a good part of my skull), you can see that we have built a fairly reasonable-looking human – even if she does have three boobs. Or he; I don't want to mischaracterize the gender of our Frankenstein-style monster.

Although made through a macabre lens, my point is that cancer sits among my family too. The fact that I still have my mother today at age 72 is why I can chat about cancer as if I know it well. It gave me back my mum; it let me keep her despite it being in her lymph glands and her first surgery not being considered a success. Still here, she is a reminder that the Big C does not mean your cards are marked, only that fear lurks in a corner of your life and must be kept under control.

Many more of us than we hear about have had to ask the dreaded question: 'How long have I got?' I would guess your consultant explained that they couldn't really give you an answer because 'everyone reacts differently', 'there is always hope', and many people 'defy expectations' and are still bouncing around ten months after they were supposed to be dead. In these conversations, I wonder whether the consultant has a better idea than they are willing to let on and knows that the way to give you the best chance possible at life is not to give you a date for your death.

I wonder if it would make it better, if you got terminal cancer or some other such diagnosis, if there were an official end date for you.

Patient: How long have I got?

Doctor: Until February 24th at 6 pm.

There would be some relief in knowing and also some relinquishment of control or effort – because the onus is on the person with cancer to fight it, right? A person is always 'fighting cancer'; charities ask for donations to help 'fight cancer together'. But would it be so very terrible to accept your cancer and just live big instead? Would it be very wrong not to waste energy on fighting but to find fun in life instead? I have so much admiration for people with cancer who decide they will not have chemotherapy and will just have a blast with the time they have left. I hope I would have the courage to do the same.

A clear expiry date would certainly be handy for relatives and loved ones because they would know when they had to book flights and be prepared. Or, in the case of half-ass children and relatives, how long they could postpone a visit because there was no rush! Having spoken to terminally ill friends of mine, they say a definitive end date would also free them up from worrying about the next lump, ache, or pain – thinking it might be the tip towards the finish line – because they would know exactly when the finish was going to come. And if things became too shockingly awful to endure and they felt they might need to exit early (or they just weren't able to take much more of the pain they were), they'd know when the end point was specifically, and could make far better decisions based on having the facts to hand.

As I have felt this way about death for a long time, I have become an advocate for assisted suicide or end-of-life medication. I've spoken to so many people who are either terminally ill or in acute pain due to some condition, and am convinced that having a small end-of-life pill sitting in their bathroom cabinet would mean they could actually live longer. It seems counterintuitive, but knowing you have a way out and are in control of when you go actually means you can stick around a lot longer; having control is very freeing. The reason Dignitas exists, and people often have to make their way there before they are ready, is because of the fear of leaving it too late and having that choice taken away. I suspect that I have that same choice to make a little further down my road.

In the UK today the only choice you have for a terminal diagnosis is some kind of a painful death, and that is cruel. We don't allow that to happen to dogs and wouldn't expect a cat to endure it, but we ask it of people young and old with cancer or wasting disease. The end-point for my friends with stomach- or bowel-cancer is crap, in every sense of the word. I'd be stashing morphine and dating a vet faster than you could say 'Sod this for a game of marbles!' Why a vet? Vets have access to the stuff you need to exit in a heady mix of joy and sleep.

At the age of 40 I was given two years to live. The actual phrase used in front of my husband and me, sitting in a room at the National Hospital for Neurology with three wise men – not in a Nativity sense; there was no gold or myrrh or baby born to a virgin involved – was, 'You will have a life-ending seizure within the next two years.' It was a big line and it was delivered well. When I look back, I really admire the guy who landed it – he said it as if he were letting me know that my flight had been canceled and I would need to reschedule. I remember everything in that room: the feel of the green chairs, the way the window blinds fell at a wonky angle, and the sudden feeling of how far I seemed to be from the door. I remember definitely not looking at my husband – I knew that one look at him and I would lose it. I had to hold it until I could get outside.

Being told you will have a life-ending epileptic fit within two years is a weird moment in your life. The bit inside of me that finds the fun in everything was wondering if it might happen there and then, so as to prove that they were not only right but also a little bit wrong: 'You said two years, bah! Watch this!'

The more honest me just about got outside and then fell apart on the pavement in my husband's arms. I sobbed like a stuck thing, and sobbed and sobbed and sobbed – for the cruelty of it all, the missing of my children's lives, the truth I knew but suddenly was told, all of the pain, and having to live more of this life only for it to be taken away without warning.

Did I feel sorry for myself? I don't think 'sorry' comes close – I felt like I was drowning in my sadness for myself. Life teaches us to be ashamed of self-pity, but there are moments when you have to open up the dam and let it all flood out. I did that in the little sadness garden they have opposite the hospital specifically for people who think they are about to die, be sick, or shit themselves. I nearly did all three.

The odd thing about being told my epilepsy would kill me within two years was not knowing the 'when'. It's a bit like terminal C, but with terminal C you're on a road with a dead end, figuratively and literally. Mine was more of a light switch – one day, someone would just reach in and turn it off.

Neither is ideal! At this point in my odd little life my seizures were always at night, brought on by my brain pattern during sleep. So all I knew was that when the end came, it was going to come at night, and it was going to be next to my husband in bed or in a hotel room on my own. Either way, I did have some serious concerns about my pajamas and nightwear. I'm not being flippant – these really are the sorts of things that those of us waiting on a death row of our body's making think about.

I did think about it from time to time, never in the day, only ever at night. Sometimes I would lie awake, fearing the sleep and the seizures it would bring – maybe one massive one that would turn my lights off for good. Every single morning when I awoke, I would text 'still here' to my mum and my husband, a secret nod to the fact that the night just gone by was not The One.

There were close shaves. As I would eventually 'come around' from a seizure, I would usually get my hearing back first, then sight, then whatever movement was available (my arms used to dislocate from their shoulder sockets), and then some kind of memory, although never enough. When ambulance crews asked me my name or what month it was, I wouldn't know the answer – and that used to make me weep every single time because I looked so stupid.

I remember one night when I could see Lovely Mark's face and knew something was really wrong, even before I knew I had had a seizure and nearly bitten through my tongue. My first thought was, what was wrong with my husband and had something happened to the children? As I started to connect the dots, I figured out that it was the middle of the night, we were in our bed, there was blood everywhere, and my arms were out of their sockets. But still, Lovely Mark looked more terrified than I could justify.

'I thought you were gone. I thought you weren't coming back.'

And that was the weirdest thing for him. My body would have all its vital signs – heartbeat, breathing, warmth – but I wouldn't be there. My brain would shut down and all of me with it; there would be just a body and eyes rolled back in their sockets. And this was his wife and the mother of his son.

Sometimes, I wondered if not coming back would be kinder to all of us. I wished for it on occasion – the pain and hurt were so great that I would wish the seizure had just taken me and let me be done.

I know that my terminal friends feel the same way. If we were to be hit by a bus, the end would be the same but without all the hurt in the middle – and without all the endless thinking about yourself, your head, how you feel, or whether you are well. Sometimes you don't even want to escape your cancer or your epilepsy – you just want to escape your own head.

Many people tell me they feel they have no one to share how they really feel with – the pain, the procedures, the aches, the hurt, all things that somehow have to be borne without being shared, or at least not easily so. It makes you question friendships that have been a lifetime in the making; most don't really want to know how you are or hear about the weird thing going on in your armpit today. Some act as if they will catch your cancer if they talk about it for too long or spend too much time with you. Few take the load.

I think it's a death thing. Once you have your terminal diagnosis, your being around is a bit like trying to have a drink with the Grim Reaper, except that you are the one with the scythe. Your friends are trying desperately hard to act like the scythe isn't there or you aren't not going to be there sooner rather than later. You have stopped being their mate Harriet and have become their friend Harriet-The -One-With-Terminal-Cancer – you and your cancer now move as one, and you bring death row with you whether you like it or not.

I hid my epilepsy and everything about it for the longest

time. It was just a more tolerable way of trying to live a normal life, by hiding the intolerable bit of my reality. My parents were scared and didn't want to know. I knew that my seizures were weird things to watch, so I never wanted a friend to see me that way. Going to A&E / E.R. in the middle of the night to have my arms relocated was not something I could drop into a conversation.

At times it would make me angry. When my mum would ask me how I was but not really want to hear anything other than 'great', I'd feel like yelling, 'How the fuck do you think I am feeling? I dislocated both my arms in the night; I puked in the car on the way home, from the drugs; my throat has had a tube shoved down it; and my mouth is an ulcerated mess. How the fuck do you think I am?' But 'great' was always the right reply. Anger is unkind and, however alone you are with your pain, it is not and will never be anyone else's fault.

It would be good if it were; sometimes, it would be great to have someone to blame or a shrink on tap to tell you real truths, too. I wanted to! Looking back, I would have liked to have had someone to tell other than Lovely Mark that this is too hard and I don't think I can do it anymore.

He made me do it once. Lovely Mark took me to the doctor and sat with me while I tried my best to tell the doctor that I couldn't cope. Mainly I just sobbed for myself, felt stupid, dribbled, snotted, and apologized for bothering him. I can still remember that room, the chairs, the way the light was, and how we all sat; it's another one of those still shots burned sharply into my brain.

I remember, too, the relief when the doctor said he

understood, that he was surprised I had managed to cope this long, and then prescribed more antidepressants and pain relief for my bones and ulcerated mouth and wished me good luck. It's almost as if I can still feel the kindness of that moment, as if someone had lifted a great big boulder that I had been carrying, acknowledging that it was heavy and I should put it down for a while.

I want you to have that person, too – someone who listens to you with all of their ears and heart, sees your pain, and tries to take some of it away or at least help you feel less alone with it. Being on death row is lonely; there are others out here who understand.

There is a very special kind of strength that comes with reconciling with death; knowing that the end is very close and you are powerless to stop it, is when that heavy boulder is taken from you for the last time.

I had thought about dying for a long time, going to bed each night wondering if this would be the one. I had imagined not being around anymore and was content with that. I was really glad I had said 'yes' to so many things in my life and gladder still for the naughtiest things I had done. Being certain you didn't waste your life is such a powerful thing when death feels close, and I like to think that everyone feels that way about their life in the end, whatever path they chose. Your life doesn't have to be glamorous or involve fancy things or lottery wins to make you feel you have lived the best life you could. Our life is the best life because it is ours.

Sure, there will be things you wanted to do or wish you could be around for. Not being there for my children when they needed me was the hardest bit, and knowing they would have sadness I couldn't cuddle away. I wondered if I should have tried cocaine at least once, and would really like to have seen what partners my children ended up with, but mostly I felt glad for all the stuff I had gotten to do in my life.

Perhaps you are scared of the end bit, still? Worried there might be pain, you won't know where you are or what's going on, or that it will be scary right at the point when you leave your body behind? I do not believe that is true. When I headed in for my surgery to try to save me, I believed it would be the end. I hoped that I might make it back, but I didn't want to if I weren't me or couldn't walk or speak anymore. I knew there was a strong chance the surgery might not go my way, but after months of absolute fear at the thought of surgery and the terror of death, I was completely calm on the morning of the actual event.

There was nothing more I could do. I didn't have to make any more decisions, didn't have to take any more pain, wouldn't spend another night waiting for my seizures, wouldn't have to pretend to be okay for anyone anymore, and I was perfectly at ease. I had lived a good life, and this end would be okay too.

It is not the same as having terminal cancer. No one's illness, pain, or death is the same, not even if it is supposed to be from the same thing. We all walk our own path, but having been as close as it is possible to get without being gone, I feel with certainty that the end is nothing to fear. Sometimes, when I am walking on a beach and the sun is so bright that everything seems white, I get that same feeling: complete calm and handing myself over to something more powerful than myself that will take care of everything from here.

There is no reason to be afraid. There is only a conversation with yourself about letting go and handing over the controls of your life to others who have you in their care. Fear is part of the fight you put up but once you stop fighting, you let go of the fear too. I got to come back from the edge of my life and was somehow reborn, seizure-free, and my life has more freedom than I ever knew because of it. I live utterly without fear now.

I talk to my children about what I want to happen when I go for the long sleep. I want my ashes put somewhere hot and dry. I do not want to be put in cold water as I hate swimming in the sea at the best of times.

I want a little plaque on my tree they are obliged to plant: 'Katie Hopkins: She died standing up.' And I hope to do exactly that; if I die lying on my ass in a hospice, I am going to be mighty cross.

Death does not define us; it is just one moment. Your life is what makes you and goes on – all the fun times, the laughter in the park, the dancing on the tables, the tears shared at hard stuff, and the pain of childbirth or broken limbs. Your life is a million moments long, and this is just one of them. Through those million moments, we all live on.

CHAPTER 15

HELP,
HOW THE HELL DID YOU
DO THAT?

I have never been a big fan of rules. Even as a little kid I thought the poolside rules at our local swimming pool were miserable: no running, no petting, no dive-bombing, no splashing.

Asking youngsters to not piss in the water would be a far more noble and worthwhile exercise than stopping a couple of kids from sneaking a cheeky snog.

I have always charted my own course and prefer to see rules and even laws as being 'advisory', as opposed to something mandated by some fat bloke in a suit. I tell my kids the same when we are driving down a road that clearly says ROAD CLOSED, or walking down a path that says NO ENTRY. I remind them these signs are just advisory.

My heart sinks when I hear someone ask if they are allowed to do such and such, or 'what's the rule?' for this or that, because that means you are already starting from the wrong place. You are already starting from the point of thinking you need to have permission to do something. It's like lining up for a 100-meter race and starting behind the blocks with no damned running shoes or sports bra: you don't stand a chance.

In this new, crazy world you can no longer ask, 'Please, may

I?' It has to be, ' Here I go; try stopping me.'

To survive this crazy little thing called life you have to at least start in the right place – which is significantly ahead of the rest of the dullards you are surrounded by. Most importantly, you have to see yourself as a free individual, blessed with the God-given rights to life, liberty, and the pursuit of happiness. This is fundamental. Frankly I don't care if you are American, a raging feminist, or identify as a gender-free squid on Wednesdays – understanding that you are born free is the only starting point that makes any sense.

You are born with these rights inside you, and anything and everything imposed on you over and above these is, by definition, a fabrication of man and therefore fundamentally flawed.

Men are imperfect things – as are women, for that matter. Every time man comes in to try to rectify a problem, he creates another. One example is the Cane Toad plagues in Australia. Introduced to control a pest problem, the toads themselves are now the pest, and driving over them in northern Australian towns is a deeply unpleasant and messy experience. When we try to fix stuff, often we simply create another problem. The same with rules: if you make up a rule, you then need someone to police it or enforce it.

I present to you the little cretin who goes around putting penalty notices on cars parked somewhere for two minutes longer than it says on the meter. No one wants to be that cretin.

If we can agree that our starting line is our right to life, liberty, and the pursuit of happiness, then we are at least approaching the starting line together, and our ability to see straight to the finish line without being impeded by nonsense is greatly enhanced.

And from this starting point, my friends, perhaps we can also agree that the time for asking permission is OVER and the time for waiting to be told an answer is THROUGH.

Covid and the regulations imposed on so many of us have violated just about every freedom we were born with. It is not hard to see why so many believe Covid to be a man-made pandemic, created in a lab and released according to a world plan to steal freedom from the people and make the world an utterly compliant place in which the masses are regulated via a social-credit system completely controlled by the ultra-elite few.

My reaction to this has been somewhat typical of my lifelong reaction to being told what to do: I have resisted and refused. More than that, I have been a bit 'extra' in most of my behavior, partly out of sheer bloody-mindedness, partly for my own sanity, and partly to signal to others that caving-in and complying are not the only options – and certainly not the solution. It sits alongside my sense of duty to stand up for my country and others afflicted by tyranny.

It's not a calculated thing on my behalf; I don't sit in my pajamas on the couch at home and think, 'What can I do to help lead people out of this abyss?' It's more that everything inside of me is raging against the madness, and I need to let it vent – verbally, physically, or emotionally. I can't NOT do anything; I have to do something. And I have to say something.

Sometimes my boldness works better for me than at others.

There have been significant moments in my adult life when I have found myself waking up in a room I did not recognize, or trying to vomit into a moving-train toilet, and realizing the error of my decision-making. True in South Africa too, where it appeared as though I was going to be taken to a police cell in Johannesburg and my future did not look too certain. True also in Australia, where I was told I was being taken to Immigration Detention for mocking that country's lockdown laws, and was eventually deported.

But for the most part, my silent scream at humanity has had some pretty awesome side effects – as illustrated perfectly by my adventure across America in Spring 2021.

Breaking into the USA

Sitting through lockdown for a good eight or nine months in the UK, I knew I had to make a break to get out of the country and head for the Land of the Free. There was no particular incentive, no particular date, and no particular reason. But I really place faith in my heart – and the way to silently scream my way out of a British lockdown and demonstrate that I was not being compliant was to make a break for America.

My aim was to demonstrate the art of the possible – and to give American audiences a reason to gather and feel better.

On March 6, 2021 that's exactly what I did.

I harnessed my freedom to life, liberty, and the pursuit of happiness, packed a single suitcase for a trip whose destination and duration were uncertain, and headed out the door. I was aiming for Colorado in the USA, where a lovely patriot and fellow freedom-fighter, Regina, was willing to take a risk on me and organize a series of events on the basis that I would actually make it into the States. Colorado was my target, and I set my sights on arriving there by the end of March 2021.

At this point it was illegal to leave the UK to go on holiday, illegal to travel, against the law to be more than seven miles from your home address, and Brits were banned from the USA. As I write this (six months later), we are still banned.

I walked out of my home on March 8. My husband and I knew this could all go south pretty fast. There were so many stop signs and so many obstacles in my way that this plan could have failed at any point. Plus, I am me, and being Katie Hopkins in the UK is not necessarily without its own set of issues.

Despite my assertions to my family and three children that I could well be back home in a couple of days, we all silently acknowledged that the last time I had said that exact phrase I wasn't home for three months – as I threw myself onto the road to campaign for President Trump.

This is not to say that any of this is easy, or somehow easier for me. Walking away from my family – teenage girls and a young son – is never easy, and certainly not easier because 'I am Katie Hopkins'. Many assume it is somehow 'easy' for me because I am an 'international celebrity'.

Hopkins Haters believed this trip would be easy for me because I am a bad mum or a heartless bitch and it doesn't hurt to leave my family behind. Some think I have a private jet or a team of staff smoothing my path. Others allege that my trip is easier for me because I am obviously being paid to do it, or because I have a magic visa that lets me into any country on the planet without proper process. Some allege that I am on the payroll of Russia or Mossad; some even boldly announce that I am with MI5 and the 'controlled opposition'.

None of the above is true, of course. There is no funding in place for me to do this stuff; it is just me, a whole bunch of cheap flights and dodgy Airbnbs, and a lot of discomfort.

The criticism I face, or the idea it is 'easy for me', is really just someone else trying to avoid taking responsibility for themselves. I used to get this a lot when I criticized overweight people. People would say that it was 'easy' for me because I am 'skinny'. If it is somehow magically 'easier' for me, then it makes the person wishing they had the balls to do the same feel better about themselves – and feel less guilty about their own lack of action.

Many ask me how I do it. There is no step-by-step instruction book. I can't tell you to get this ticket, this piece of paper, and book this or that hotel; it is not like that.

It is absolutely a mindset. It is 100 percent in your heart that you are going to do this thing and you will find a way, whatever it takes. I think it is only 'easier for me' in the sense that it is my calling. I have no choice BUT to do this because I think this is what I was put here on this crazy planet to do.

I am not saying my path is for everyone. I am not suggesting for one moment that others should feel the calling to do what I do and abandon their family for a crazy mission to the States. I'm simply stating that it is not easier for me.

I own my determination to do it. It's the same reason that I put on 50 pounds in three months and lost it again in three months: to challenge the people who said I had no right to an opinion about those who are overweight because it is 'easy' for me because I am 'skinny'. So I made myself obese to ram the point home. Even then, people tried to argue that it was 'easier' for me because I don't have a medical condition (overlooking my killer epilepsy and the bucket loads of meds I used to take at that time). Some people are just so used to making excuses for themselves that they can't stop.

I also appreciate that achieving these weirdly extraordinary things makes me even more annoying to my critics. But it makes me very comfortable with who I am. I am absolutely true to my beliefs; I mean what I say; and I own my decisions and the outcomes, good and bad.

The world around you can feel very out of control, but being comfortable with yourself is completely within your purview (this is a great word) and one of the most powerful tools you have.

Oddly, I was very comfortable with myself even when I was the most hated woman in Britain – and, for many, I still am. I think it helps to explain how I was able to handle so much hate. There was, and is, an enormous distance between who I know I am and the hated woman others think they know.

I am also acutely aware that the nightmares of lockdowns and of governments willing to impose immeasurable cruelty on their own people have helped people to see what I am trying to do and to acknowledge I have been crucified by the state and the media for my determination to be true to myself and the people whose stories I was trying to tell.

Lockdowns and the malice of tyrannical governments willing to hurt their own people have made me scream harder than at any time in my past. They have made my body scream physically (hence my arms and abs); they have made my heart scream emotionally. And as for rationality, forget it; there is nothing rational about any of this. I am perfectly clear with myself: the time for asking for permission is over, and the time for waiting for an answer is through.

Let's go back to the day I left to make my break for America. As I walked away from my family and my home, all of the following were absolutely true:

- It is illegal to go on a vacation.
- It is illegal to be more than seven miles from your home address.
- It is illegal to leave the UK unless you are on essential work, narrowly defined.
- It is illegal for British people to travel to America.
- No visas are being issued or accepted by the U.S. embassy, which remains closed.
- British people are banned from U.S. by the Biden administration, and have been for a year.
- I am not being paid to do any of this.
- No one specifically asked me to make the journey.
- Failure is far much more likely than success. Both options will be expensive.
- I am Katie Hopkins, 'The Biggest Bitch in Britain', and that is not always helpful.

I stepped out of my door, hauled my staircase onto a train (an unapproved journey), and made my break for the USA.

Step One: Get out of Britain

Family aside, the decision to leave the UK was not a difficult one.

We had been locked down hard for over a year; our kids had

been shoved out of school; we were banned from being more than seven miles from our home address; and neighbors were busily reporting neighbors for any infringement of the rules. The only things keeping me in the country were my husband, my children, my elderly parents, and my sense of duty. Under Covid, the UK had grown cruel, spiteful, and increasingly small.

To get to America, I first needed to find a way out of the UK.

Given that holidays were no longer allowed, I could not find a route through a popular holiday destination. I had used this tactic in the past; because British people were banned from the States, I had journeyed to Barbados, cleansed myself of being British by camping out there for 20 days, and then snuck onto one of the last Jet Blue flights from Barbados to the USA. But this was no longer an option.

So I chose Germany. I chose it because no British person really wants to go to Germany. Its people are utterly devoid of personality; their language is so guttural it makes you sound like you are committing manslaughter with every sentence; and its leader for the last 15 years or so has been the rotund ginger lesbian Angela Merkel, who has never had a child – which, frankly, is a blessing on their unborn souls.

Angela Merkel could murder both her parents in the night with an ice pick and still turn up in a pantsuit at the European Union by 7am to discuss fisheries policy, barely pausing to wipe off a bit of brain matter from behind her left ear. She is that level of autistic, and she runs the whole damned country. I have often thought that Merkel and the tennis player Djokovic should get together because they are as emotionally void as each other. Maybe if you put two extreme psychopaths in a room together they will cancel each other out and create some kind of thermonuclear lovefest. Or maybe not.

As an example of just how weird they are, Germans don't have turnstiles at the Metro or train station, but they buy their tickets without fail because they are supposed to, because it is the rule. And if it is the rule, you do it. (Try saying this with a comedic German accent; it is way funnier.)

In Germany you can be fined for walking across the road at the wrong angle. You have to cross a road at 90 degrees; if you are off with your goddamned protractor and cross at 70 degrees or less, you can (and probably will) be given a fine.

Remember, I believe that rules are advisory. When I was in that country and dared to cross the road before the walking man turned green, Germans looked at me as if I had just raped a small farm animal. That level of violation just doesn't happen in Germany. I like to remind their little shocked faces that we won the war – twice.

It's not so much that they are on the spectrum; as we agreed in Chapter 8, the spectrum is a great place to be. It's more that they are set to operate in binary numerics.

This level of autism would be the perfect cover for my break to America because, as a journalist, what could be more spine-crushingly tedious than going to Frankfurt? Only a real journalist on essential business could be asked to do that, surely.

Happily, the guy at the airline check-in desk was Indian, a massive bonus because the Indian diaspora typically loves me, Despite turning away the couple in front of me who needed to get to a funeral, he accepted my trip as essential and waved me through.

Step Two: PCR testing at Heathrow Airport

In order to get on any plane out of the UK – if you are among the tiny handful of people actually allowed to get onto a plane to go somewhere – you need a PCR test. (I am praying that by the time you read these words this will no longer be true, but I have a horrible feeling that this draconian rule will still be in place.)

The reasons why PCR testing is ridiculous are too numerous to put down on paper, but the test is bullshit. Also, the sensitivity of the test can be manipulated to make the result positive or negative; one gentleman secured a positive result by dipping his swab in a can of Coke. A mango can give you a positive PCR test. Essentially, if a scientist wants more positive test results, he or she can make it so simply by making the test more sensitive to Covid markers.

I paid $150.00 for the privilege of this crap, not because I believe in it but because I needed the bit of paper to even try to get onto the plane. Hardcore freedom-lovers rage at me for 'complying' with these tests. They don't get it: I have a clear aim and sometimes you have to make sacrifices to achieve that.

In fact, my test was worth every damned penny. As it turned out, the ambulance lady performing my test in the cubicle, dressed in full Emergency Responder gear, was a Katie Hopkins fan.

I walked in; she shut the door, closed the curtain, and gave me the biggest hug from a stranger I had enjoyed in a long while. Then she trotted off and got 'Julie' from cubicle 4 because she was also a supporter, and we all took selfies together.

They acknowledged that testing and all of the Covid crap was nonsense and that none of it made any sense. These lovely ladies sitting inside the NHS have to comply because they need their paychecks and their pensions. It is all an insult to their intelligence, their skills, and their endeavor.

I think this also demonstrates why people paid by the state are so much easier to control, and therefore how tragic it is to see that we are headed on a trajectory towards Universal Basic Income – i.e. everyone being paid by the state.

'Furlough' is a precursor to this. During lockdown 80 percent of British workers were being paid by the state. Once the state has its tentacles around people's incomes and their ability to pay their mortgages, or, indeed, feed their families, they have full control.

Either way, I walked out of the airport test center with a negative Covid test certificate and onto a plane to Germany. After eight months of perpetual lockdown and pretending to be a mum and wife nearly 24/7, I had finally left the UK.

Step Three: Frankfurt to somewhere

Frankfurt did not disappoint. 'Due to Covid' is a phrase that has been abused for everything from snacks and drinks on a plane to not allowing my daughter to borrow a library book. Now, 'due to Covid', I was obliged to stay inside the airport terminal building for 30 hours to wait for my connection to Mexico; I was not allowed to enter Germany proper.

So now I was Tom Hanks/Viktor Navorski (from the movie The Terminal, in which Tom/Viktor lives as a man with no country in the airport terminal building at JFK for the best part of a year) – not officially allowed to have left the UK, not allowed to enter Germany, and yet here just the same. I was a non-person, in a non-place.

Step Four: Cleansing myself of being British

Now I needed a country to hide in to cleanse myself of being British. Along with all the rules and regulations about why a British person could not be in the U.S., there was one killer: In order for a Brit (or anyone from the Euro or Schengen Zone) to enter the U.S., they must not have been in the UK (or Schengen Zone) for the previous 15 days.

I needed to cleanse myself of being British. I needed to have been 'somewhere else' for 15 days, and that somewhere else needed to be somewhere acceptable to the USA.

Bullshit Covid-19 Rule 254 states that 'it is illegal for a British person to go on holiday'. I needed to go somewhere that only an absolutely ESSENTIAL worker would go under significant duress.

Bullshit Covid-19 Rule 294 states that 'most countries on the planet are red countries and will not accept Brits, particularly not Katie Hopkins'. I needed a country NOT on the red list and DESPERATE enough to accept me.

And there it was, a shining beacon of 'not giving a shit-ness' on a hill of excrement built by politicians and bureaucrats with nothing better to do than piss on people's chips. A city that kills more journalists than any other city on the face of the planet, in a country that puts the fear of God into most Westerners. Mexico City!

Step Five: Frankfurt to Mexico City

I hopped onto my plane like a bunny with extra legs. Germany was delighted to see its very own Tom Hanks leave the terminal building; I was elated to be out of that infernal country, and knew that my chances of a successful break into America had just increased exponentially.

Mostly, I was glad to be leaving German people behind. I am always terrified that some of their seriousness will rub off on me by weird autistic osmosis.

There are snags that I am brushing over, of course. A journey that would normally look like an 8-to-10- hour flight across the Atlantic was rapidly turning into an expensive 25-day epic marathon involving more miles, painful hours in economy seats, and dodgy accommodations than I care to mention. This was a test of endurance.

The costs were horrible too. At a time when there is no competition, companies can charge whatever they like, and I don't get to charge expenses to anyone but myself. The struggle to find cafes or bathrooms to eat in or take a pee in (respectively) was relentless. No normal person with a home, family, and no financial incentive would put themselves through this.

It is not that I am oblivious to risk, either.

I had done my research on Mexico City with contacts and travelers from the road, and had spoken to the handful of people I trust. Even strong military men and others working in high-level security had some reservations. Most had stories of a mugging or robbery, and females were a write-off, saying they wouldn't go near the place even if I paid them.

I understood their fears, and they were all well-founded.

But, sometimes, asking for the opinion of others is futile. You have to follow your heart and trust in your skills. Ultimately, I am still me; I am not built the way others are, and I trust myself and am confident of myself on the road. I walk mean streets as if I belong there, or become invisible as if I were never there. As they say of aged hookers in Philadelphia, this was not 'my first rodeo', and I came prepared for the ride.

Step Six: Mexico City - Tulum - Puerto Morelos

Mexico City is fantastic and turned out to be an amazing adventure. They waved me through immigration with smiles and gratitude; a trusty driver from my hotel came to collect me and was delightful; and my hotel (booked for £65 per night) was a kind of Grand Palace with an elaborate glass ceiling and palatial flooring. It was the Grand Hotel Budapest, or luxury Rome, its former glory woven into its seams. I fell in love immediately.

Mexico is everything lockdown Britain is not: bustling, thriving, defiant, and pulsating with life. There is a determination in these people to prevail – there damned well has to be if they are going to make it in a country where the average income is less than 120 pesos per day (about $8).

The market traders crowd together in alleyways; the illegal traders spread their wares on blankets tied with string that can be snapped up and hidden from inspectors at a moment's notice; and the food vendors are all about.

In the cheap-clothing department of fashion stores near the main square, the security woman has a semi-automatic weapon, and no one gets out of the store without showing a receipt for every item purchased or being shot – which is a simple but effective strategy for protecting stock.

I ran through the back alleyways and less well-trodden places on my morning run, loving all of it – the piss, the poverty, the determination to prevail. I find life in the raw incredibly uplifting; I always have.

One morning I took a fall, a fairly heavy one, and came smashing to the ground. I even had time to think, 'Sh*t, this isn't smart,' before I landed. Two gentlemen came to scoop me up from the road, asking if I was okay and checking my bleeding knees, and offered me drugs to make me feel better. I love these Mexican men for their kindness.

Families here have it the right way, too. Towards the coast and the Port of Morelos, the church is at the center of a tiny fishing village, its doors flung open and flowers spilling out from each pew. On a Sunday the local beach fills with Mexican families, the great grandmothers awarded a special chair of their own, the rest of the family crowding around her, 15 to 20 strong from the oldest to the tiniest baby, who looks like he may have been birthed on the sidewalk or the walk down to the beach. These families have little money, no phones, no gadgets, and no distractions, but they are endlessly jolly, filling up the empty spaces of life we fill with stuff that subtracts from our family with stuff that builds up their family instead: laughter, love, and food.

I rang my husband and told him we needed to move the family to Mexico, immediately. I met plenty of others doing just the same. Well-heeled Californians, who had headed here to this quiet place to escape the tyranny of Democratic governors, had put their stuff into storage and were not planning to return. Mexico is a simpler and better way of life. I acknowledge that this comes from the perspective of someone with funds. A Westerner of average means is a millionaire in a country where most have nothing. I see that part of this is my (colorless) privilege talking. But they have much more than us in so many ways.

Of course, they had Covid and the requirement to wear a mask. But at no time did anyone ever ask or question me regarding a mask. At no point did anyone wear it as a badge of honor. And at no time would anyone tell a Mexican not to work, because without work they don't eat. It's not even a conversation.

Control is harder to achieve when decent people have to attend to the basic needs of life. I told my family that even if I failed to get into America, I would always be proud to have spent time with these beautiful people. Had I been turned back from this place to the UK, I would not have regretted my trip, spending my sunny days penning this book and loving the absolute simplicity of my life here – and the salted margaritas, of course.

Step Seven: Mexico City to the USA

My attempt to break back into the U.S. was only possible because of the longstanding media visa in my passport, absolutely the best thing to have come out of working for The Daily Mail. All other visas and ESTAS had been annulled by the U.S.'s embassies, so, in part, my path was only even potentially possible due to a visa I had acquired years before the Covid nightmare.

As with every other leg of this trip, I needed to find out the rules and somehow beat them all to advance into the States.

I had cleansed myself of being British courtesy of 20 days in Mexico: tick. I had a journalist visa that was still in date: tick. Now I needed yet another PCR test, so I set off to purchase a negative Covid-19 certificate from Alejandro on the beach in Mexico for 20 pesos: tick.

The great thing about Mexicans is, if there is an opportunity to make money, they will find it. Pimping negative Covid-19 certificates to American tourists needing to get on a flight is essentially a license to print cash. In Mexico almost anything can be procured in exchange for some local currency, from testosterone to anabolic steroids to Viagra.

Negative Covid-19 tests are no exception.

Step Eight: The last leg

Waiting in line to check in for my flight to Colorado was my final hurdle and a thumping great moment in my life – knowing I had jumped every damned hurdle, wiggled through hoops, overturned rules, outmaneuvered the paper-pushers, met some wonderful people, and had a blast doing all of it. And I had really learned the meaning of letting go of control. The more I threw myself to the wind, the more clearly my path revealed itself. And the less I pretended to be in control, the more splendid the path I was given to walk.

Landing in the States and selecting the immigration officer who looked most like someone I would like to sleep with at a wedding was the ultimate test of my assertion that the time for asking for permission was over and the time for waiting for an answer was through. He looked at my passport. I gave him the look that told him I would definitely sleep with him at a wedding, and he stamped my passport, smiled, and said: 'Welcome home.'

I sat down by the luggage carousal and wept.

HOW TO BE A BETTER RULE BREAKER

Accept risk and failure

Breaking rules, however daft they may be, is not without

risk or the threat of failure. There are typically two things that actually hold you back. The first is not the rule itself, but the thought of the risk it exposes you to and the fear of consequence or failure. The second is that, in order to be able to decide you aren't asking anyone else for permission, you need to own not only the cool freedom part but also the consequences, the uncertainty, and the potential for things to go horribly and spectacularly wrong.

When I say I am throwing myself to the wind on these adventures, it is much more than just an expression. A real release is required – a release of all control, a release of holding onto stuff, and an acceptance that one's landing may be rough or might hurt.

I guess my baseline is that I will end up in prison. I have known and accepted this for around a decade, so you could argue that I am farther down the path than any normal person. But then, I would argue that my willingness to expose myself to hurt and hardship is what has given me my voice and my freedom. That's a transaction that has paid dividends for me in the way I get to live my life.

It is never easier for me

This is an excuse we have already addressed. When you wish to do something you have seen someone else do, you often let yourself off the hook by working out that it is 'easier' for that other person, and giving yourself a long list of excuses as to why it is 'harder' for you. Other than being an actual paraplegic, none of these excuses line up. Some of the best paraplegics I know have made it to the tops of mountains and have completed marathons.

Accept discomfort and pain

Breaking stuff is painful, whether it's bones or rules. If you are a package-holiday type who likes your transport arranged for you, a coach waiting to take you to your accommodation, and not having to make any decisions, you aren't going to be the sort of soul who likes risk. Accept pain and discomfort as your baseline and when you find yourself sitting on a beach with a raw coconut you will feel like the King of Your Own Land.

Be a magnet for conversation

I appreciate this isn't just something you can turn on with a switch. But the road is lonely and if you are like me and need human contact to feel happy, then you need to be a magnet for conversation. Reframe the way you see the world, particularly if you are British or from a Nordic country prone to looking down and keeping your mouth closed due to the freezing winds.

The fella at the check in desk, the waitress, the bar tend, the air crew – they are all people, and all have things to say other than 'Have a great day!' Brush up against their lives and have conversations along your way. When it's just you against the world, you need to be turbo charged to attract others, make like a magnet and pull them in.

Be comfortable with yourself

If you are looking for someone to tell you you are great, everything is going to be okay, or you are making the right decision, you are still reliant. You need to be able to cut the umbilical cord and become independent enough to trust yourself and to trust that you can handle the things that go wrong.

We all need someone to check in with or to call in times of doubt. We all need a rock. I have Lovely Mark, and I often call him and say, 'This happened; I think I need to do this. What's the right answer?' And we work it through. But, fundamentally, you need to be able to operate without this helpline and see that, out there on your own, no one is going to tell you you are wonderful or make your life easier. It is all on you, and you need to grow your shoulders to fill that space.

Start at the start line, not behind it

If your question is 'Where can I travel to under lockdown?' or 'Is the vaccination safe?' you are not starting at the start line. You are way behind the starting blocks, back where runners store their kit and coats. It is not your fault. Government communications and a lifetime of being told what to do schools you to think this way – to only ask the questions you are supposed to ask.

The question is not 'Where can I travel under lockdown?' but rather 'Where do I want to go?' The question is not 'What am I allowed to do?' but rather 'My freedom is my God-given right; how do I remove the thing standing in my way?' You need to take charge of your freedom and question everything that stands in its path. The only way to stay ahead is to start at the start line and to step off it with the determination to stay on your track.

Translating this into your own life

This doesn't mean you need to go and risk your safety in Mexico. It doesn't mean that prison has to be your bottom line in the same way it is mine. But if you take the essence of this thinking and apply it to your own life, if you try to throw yourself to the wind a little more every day, and really throw your arms around the best bits of it, your path will become clearer and your journey a whole lot more special.

Pick the immigration officer you would sleep with at a wedding

This is just a bloody great rule for living life.

Take time to appreciate the good stuff when it happens

I was on the road for 100 days, across three countries and four states, and spoke at over 60 events. More importantly, I helped give people a reason to gather at a time when they had never felt more alone. Grown men cried on me, wives told me of their despair, and one lady laughed so hard that she wet herself and we had to change her chair.

For a while there, I felt like we had shifted something in the matrix; somehow, the world just seemed like a better place.

CHAPTER 16

EMERGENCY HELP

Any time you doubt yourself, have just completely lost your sh*t in public, or have told your daughter / son / mother-in-law (delete as appropriate) to get the hell out of your life, have a little read of these rules for life. If nothing else, they will buy you time to recover and help you remember you are not a bad person, what just happened is not that big a deal, and you are doing the best you can.

If you are unsure what to do, breathe in and out

Do it. Right now.

I cannot tell you how many times I have been down to my last ounce of patience or will, or perhaps been in such a pickle that I thought I might just piss myself … and have reminded myself to breathe, just breathe. All the way in – and all the way out. And then do it again.

When life gets too tough, go fundamental. Breathing is about as fundamental as it gets. You gain a little time, you gain oxygen for your brain, and you get to take a moment. In that moment, you will find that extra ounce of energy you need.

Don't breathe like a little shrew that has been caught by a cat.

Breathe like a big fat mole that just popped up to the surface and intends to stand there for a while because it's sunny. Be more mole.

Remember, you are a good person

Did you just kill someone? Steal from them? Damage their belongings or sh*t on their lawn? No? So it turns out you are actually a good person and are trying to do the right thing, no matter what others or the demons in your head are trying to tell you.

Sometimes something might go a bit wrong, or you might not be the best version of yourself. Shouting 'GO FUCK YOURSELF!' at the delivery driver would be an example of this.

But it is important to cut yourself some slack and remember you are a good person and you mean well. Repeat after me: 'I am a good person, and I really want everyone to be as happy as they can possibly be.'

(If you DID just kill someone or sh*t on someone's lawn, now is probably not the time for light reading. I'd suggest legging it to Costa Rica or getting a lawyer.)

Yes, you can!

I do not wish to go all Obama on your furry ass, but our default programming is 'No, I can't.' Closely behind 'No, I can't' is the question 'What if it goes wrong, what if ... I end up naked on a table with a stapler up my ass?' (I literally have no idea where my mind goes sometimes.)

I am here to tell you – yes, TELL YOU – that yes, you can, and so what to 'what if'?

Ask yourself: 'When will I EVER get the opportunity to do this again?' Not only is it a much better question, but if it is a life-ending activity that you decide to partake in, the answer won't matter.

What use is a life if you only half live it? Say yes. Do the details later.

Be ready

Packed and ready by my desk is a rucksack with passport, card, cash, adaptors, battery charger, cables, big scarf, a toothbrush, and a five-pack of DoubleDeckers (an iconic British chocolate bar that cannot be found abroad).

I can be out the door to anywhere in five minutes and not need to come back, ever. This is a mindset as much as a bag. I strongly advise you to get yourself one.

The road is always calling me, and some of my best answers have come from it. It is a mindset of being prepared and being unafraid of change.

And if you ever need to leave your house in an emergency, you will have me to thank.

Be quiet

Us chatty types like to fill a space, and typically we find silence awkward. But, before I go on a big call or have an important conversation – particularly if it is going to be a bit awkward – I write a note to myself to speak less.

My husband tells me the same thing: hold your tongue and listen. When I receive text messages that are particularly aggressive or demanding in nature, I simply type the word 'seen'. It drives the sender crazy. They want to know what I am going to do next – and I am not going to tell them.

Those who seek to belittle you or diminish you do not deserve your words. Give them silence instead.

With friends, it is often the gaps in between life that matter most. In silence, the most interesting conversations fall out. You just have to be brave enough to let them.

Never apologize, never explain

I am not talking about your private life; obviously, Lovely Mark and I would have divorced a very long time ago if I didn't say sorry when I am a tub-thumping git.

But when it comes to your life outside your front door, this should be a first principle. Being forced into an apology only encourages the bastards, and it will never be enough to satiate their bloodlust. The mob braying for your blood will not stop until you are swinging from a tree. Your mere existence is an act of defiance.

If your heart is broken, keep crying

Eventually you will stop. And when you stop, something else will begin.

It is not surprising we fear hard decisions that are going to hurt, and it can be tempting to avoid them. I have tried avoiding terrible moments in my life. It is a fool's errand.

If you are desperately unhappy with something in your life, don't live with it or work around it. Have the courage to change it – even if it hurts. (This can apply to husbands but not to dogs – you have to keep those.)

Find the fun

It might mean you miss your plane or have some awkward explaining to do. It could well mean that one of your friends doesn't speak to you for a very long time.

But if it's fun and you want it, do it. Stop and drink a glass of wine alone at a bar while thinking good thoughts. Dance naked on your balcony. Cuddle someone for a lot longer than you should.

Guilt is overrated and pleasing others is not as important as pleasing yourself. (This does not apply to hard drugs or heroine; the fun has to be cleaner than that.)

Always be polite in an ambulance

The guys in jumpsuits working the ambulance control your access to drugs. They are the ones who do the hand over to the hospital and are your best chance of getting a decent reception when you get to A&E / E.R.

If you p*ss them off you don't stand a chance. Be respectful, try to be dignified, and, if you HAVE p*ssed yourself, apologize.

A man who makes you feel bad about yourself is not a man you need in your life

This is also true if it is a woman, although if the woman is your mother, she gets special rights.

It has to be said, my husband often makes me feel bad about my behavior, but for all the right reasons. By now I think we can all agree I can be a massive ass, and he is good enough to point this out, and I am obliged to do something about it.

But if a man really is making you feel like crap about yourself, your better self needs to step in and protect you. I have been this woman, and she withstood too much of this for too long.

For the people in your life to be happy, you need to be happy. Don't fool yourself into thinking your martyrdom will help anyone.

Swim naked

There's a reason babies are pissed off when they are born. One minute they are having a lovely swim, and the next some rough-handed midwife is rubbing them down with a cheap towel.

If you are pondering the meaning of your life, or in need of inspiration, swim naked. There is something umbilical about it and, even if it doesn't answer all the questions in your head, you will enjoy the feeling of water flowing freely about your bits.

I love it, in a slightly sexual way. And I am OK admitting it here, in print, with you.

You don't have to say yes

Just because someone asks to marry you doesn't mean you have to say yes. No is an equally acceptable answer.

Imagine yourself brave

There is a brave person inside all of us. As the expression goes, sometimes we just have to make the leap and let our wings unfurl on the way down.

Step out like you are invincible. Challenge the rest of you to catch the hell up.

I am. I can. I will. Repeat after me, I am. I can. I will.

And if the universe answers back with a beating and leaves you wasted on the floor, take time to rebuild yourself and then go again. I bloody well am. I bloody well can. I bloody well will.

You are not alone

The people who know you best love you most of all. Sometimes you just need to tell people you are hurt and how they can help you to feel okay. And if you are still looking around and seeing no one, remember that you have me.

As I tell my children repeatedly, I am right here in your pocket. I will always be here, no matter what. Whatever happens in your life, no matter what you have done, I am here to reassure you that everything is going to be okay.

Breathe in, breathe out. Remember you are a good person.

And now, go do the next thing, no matter how tiny that next thing might be.

Printed in Great Britain
by Amazon